W9-CBR-803

The Dogfather

Dog Lover's Mysteries by Susan Conant

The Dogfather

A DOG LOVER'S MYSTERY

Susan Conant

BERKLEY PRIME CRIME, NEW YORK

THE DOGFATHER

A Berkley Prime Crime Book
Published by The Berkley Publishing Group,
a division of Penguin Putnam Inc.,
375 Hudson Street, New York, New York 10014.

ISBN 0-425-18838-8

ACKNOWLEDGMENTS

For the appearance of Alaskan Malamute BISS International/AM CH Malko's Wookie of Kunek, WPD, CGC, the fabulous Mr. Wookie, I am grateful to Mary Wood. In these pages, as in real life, Mr. Wookie is accompanied and owner-handled by Mary. I am also grateful to Cindy Neely for the reappearance in my stories of CH Jazzland's Embraceable You, the beautiful Emma. My profuse congratulations to Mr. Wookie for his Best of Breed and to Emma for her Award of Merit at the 2001 Alaskan Malamute National Specialty. I also want to thank the malamute who keeps my fiction truthful, my own Rowdy, Frostfield Perfect Crime, CD, CGC, WPD, ThD.

Special thanks to the best daughter a mother has ever had, Jessica Park, for her generous, loving, and intelligent help with this book. Many thanks to Jean Berman, Thomas Davies, Roo Grobis, Amanda Kirk, Roseann Mandell, Geoff Stern, Anya Wittenborg, and Corinne Zipps, and to my marvelous editor, Natalee Rosenstein.

To my beloved grandson, Nicholas Carter Park,
and his first dog, the angelic Samantha.

CHAPTER 1

My affiliation with organized crime began a few years ago when I accidentally did a favor for a godfather named Enzio Guarini. Ignoring the serendipity of my assistance, Guarini decided that he owed me one. I disagreed, but wasn't stupid enough to say so. I live in Cambridge, Massachusetts. I like it here. My house is modest, but enjoys the tremendous advantage of being above ground. A difference of opinion with Enzio Guarini might've meant an involuntary change of residence. I didn't fancy downward mobility.

Speaking of fancy, that's what Guarini and I had in common: the Dog Fancy, together with associated nuttiness on the subject of all dogs everywhere and outright lunacy when it came to our own. Our differences? Where to begin? With age, sex, and money. The elderly male

Guarini presided over an empire of legitimate enterprises that included a pasta factory, a construction business, a trucking company, and a wholesale liquor distributorship. He was, however, reported to profit from criminal activities such as loan sharking, drug trafficking, gambling, prostitution, and money laundering. I, in contrast, am a mid-thirties female exclusively engaged in the ultralegitimate, if somewhat less than lucrative, fields of professional dog writing and dog training. My idea of money laundering is accidentally leaving a one-dollar bill in the pocket of my jeans when I throw them in the wash. For what it's worth, I must add that Guarini was reputed to have killed so many people that even the FBI had lost count; he was universally regarded as a man of extreme violence. In contrast, the thousands of victims of my own murderous binges have consisted of insects that threatened the health and comfort of my dogs. If you ask people about me, what you're going to hear is, *Holly Winter? Oh, she wouldn't hurt a flea.* Whether Guarini's reputation and mine are deserved, you'll have to judge for yourself.

To backtrack.

One evening in mid-April, the dogs and I were harmlessly wending our way home from a walk to Harvard Square, home being the three-story barn-red house at the corner of Appleton and Concord, and the dogs being exemplary specimens of the breed of breeds, fire of the tundra, strength of strengths, light of the Polar night, and light of the life of Holly Winter, the justifiably legendary Wild Dog of the North, the noble and glorious Alaskan malamute.

You *did* ask whether I had any pets, didn't you? Three, as it happens, a cat named Tracker and two dogs, Alaskan malamutes, Rowdy and Kimi, about whom I could go on, as I often have and certainly will and, moreover, would do so right now at tremendous length and in excruciating detail except that I've got a story to tell. To resume, we were unexpectedly interrupted in our harmless wending of our unobjectionable way homeward up Concord Avenue by the appearance of a somewhat old-fashioned black limousine that snuck up on us, slunk along beside us, and thus stalked us in what struck me as catlike fashion for a few yards before it crept ahead and came to an ominous halt at the curb. Its tinted windows gave it an aura of inscrutability, and the almost inaudible sound of its engine was the distinctive, growling purr of a cat who's about to sink his teeth into the flesh at the base of your thumb. Whether Rowdy and Kimi shared my sense of feline threat I can't say. When it came to cats, they were more threat than threatened, and in any case, they not only considered themselves the toughest guys on our block, but honestly were.

The passenger-side front door of the limo flew open to disgorge a man so vertically and horizontally gigantic that he almost blocked the sidewalk ahead of us. His mountainous proportions alone would've startled me. As to his features, you know that anthropological debate about whether modern homo sapiens is part Neanderthal? A glance at this guy's brow ridge and prognathic jaw settled the question in my mind, although that wasn't, of course, the question of immediate concern to me at the time, and for obvious reasons, I didn't try to settle the academic one by asking the brute whether his immediate ancestors had worn loin cloths and fashioned primitive tools out of stone. The creature blocking our path had, I might mention, exceptionally pale skin and dark hair, and wore twenty-first-century men's pants and a zippered jacket that looked as if it should've had a candlepin logo on the breast and the name of a bowling league embroidered across the back.

The dogs and I came to a halt. Only then did I notice that the limo had pulled over under a street light and that Alley Oop was taking advantage of the illumination to peer at Rowdy, Kimi, and me through narrowed and depthlessly stupid eyes. These are show dogs, so they're used to being scrutinized. They love it. And even if I didn't show my dogs, they'd still get stared at because they're big, wolflike, and show-offy, so our neighborhood strolls are punctuated by dog-admiration pauses. But I *do* show my dogs. I'd be a fool not to. They're gorgeous. Anyway, Rowdy and Kimi have been trained to gait beautifully and to pose handsomely before American Kennel Club judges, which was more or less what they were doing right now, free-stacking rather than wiggling all over, hurling themselves onto the ground, and rolling onto their backs in the hope of tummy rubs, the way they did in sidewalk mode. The dogs showed not a trace of their rare and subtle response to a perceived threat to their beloved biped companion, which in Kimi's case consisted of sitting vigilantly at my side and in Rowdy's, of transforming himself into a furry brick wall by stationing himself between me and the potential aggressor. Indeed, the only participant in the encounter who demonstrated unusual behavior was the colossal man: His gaze took in both my dogs and me.

Having evidently reached some decision about the three of us, the hulk turned back toward the limo door, which had remained ajar, and uttered an affirmative grunt. As I was trying to remember whether Neanderthals were believed capable of language, the limo's rear door opened, and out stepped a second man. He was shorter than the first and strikingly narrow, with sloping shoulders, a stretched out neck, an ax-shaped head, dark hair, and a prominent widow's peak.

He jabbed a hand in my direction, then pointed an extraordinarily elongated index finger toward the interior of the limousine. Leaving no question about the language capacity of vampires, he said, "The boss wants to see you." His voice was adenoidal and squeaky, but unlike movie mobsters, he pronounced *the* and *to* in ordinary fashion instead of reducing the words to *duh*.

"The boss," I echoed. Pointing a normal-size index finger at my big dogs, I said, "Around here, *the boss* means me." Then I stalled for time. Concord Avenue is not only a busy street, but my street, and in this academic community of sensible vehicles, the limo stood out like a raven among house sparrows. With luck, my next-door neighbor Kevin Dennehy would drive by. If he did, he'd notice the limo, the dogs, and me. Kevin is a Cambridge police lieutenant. He notices everything, wonders what's up, and always finds out. "But I take it that you mean someone other than me," I prattled. "My father might possibly see himself as someone's boss, but probably not mine. He knows me better than that. We go back a few years. Then there's my editor, Bonnie, but we communicate by phone and E-mail, and if *Dog's Life* magazine is springing for a limo, it's a first. So I guess you must be talking about *your* boss. Is that right?"

I ran my eyes up and down Concord Avenue. Kevin Dennehy was nowhere in sight. Unfortunately, while I was scanning the street, Kimi took advantage of my meandering gaze to apply her own coplike observational skills. Worse, in Kevin-like fashion, my observant Kimi acted, which is to say that one second she was standing politely on a loose lead, and the very next second, she was practically tearing my arm out of its socket by lunging through the open rear door of the limousine and into its dimly lit interior. In an apparent effort to disjoint my other arm, Rowdy hurled himself after her. Dutifully maintaining my grip on the dogs' leashes, I flew through the air, whacked my shins, smashed my head, and tumbled into the limo and thus into a roaring dog fight. The dogs had taken over the rear seat, and I landed ignominiously on the floor. At the edge of my vision and consciousness, I was aware that Count Dracula and the caveman now occupied the rear-facing seat, and that the limo was moving. Still, I felt oddly buoyed by the need to deal with an immediate problem that I knew how to resolve. Sure, we'd been shanghaied, but so what? I knew how to break up the fight and could probably restore peace without getting bitten.

Rowdy, my male, and the larger of the two dogs, had leaped right on top of Kimi and now had her pinned. Kimi's head was tucked down in what I felt sure was an effort to protect whatever edible treasure had impelled her to jump into the limo in the first place. How did I know it was edible? Because I know my Kimi. Her determination to maintain possession of her booty impeded her ability to rid herself of Rowdy, whose jaws were locked on the skin at the back of her neck. Both dogs issued deep, throaty growls. In the rare battles that occur between Rowdy and Kimi, hideous rumbling and yelping are actually a good sign. With luck, the dogs pierce the air instead of rending each other's flesh.

I sprang to the rear seat, kneeled, and bellowed orders. "Rowdy, enough! Leave it!" Wrapping my left hand around his rolled-leather collar, I shoved the fingers of my right hand into that spot between the molars and the temporomandibular joint. "Let go!" Switching to a happy tone of voice, I caroled, "Rowdy, watch me right now!"

Ten zillion hours of obedience training, and I'm always stunned when the dog obeys. I could feel Rowdy's head turn slightly. As his jaws loosened their grip, I yanked him off Kimi and then dragged him across the luxurious carpet and up onto the opposite seat, where I planted him between the surprised Neanderthal and the amazed vampire. Rowdy weighed only a bit over eighty-five pounds, but his thick double coat combined with his weighty manner created the illusion of tremendous size. Even so, had the rear-facing seat been one of those flimsy fold-down affairs, it would've collapsed under Rowdy and the two men. Fortunately, it was a full bench seat. Not that getting abducted in any limousine is exactly fortunate, but better in a luxury limo than in some cut-rate job, I guess.

Addressing the vampire, I said, "*You!* Grab the dog's collar and hang on to it. His name is Rowdy. He's a good dog. He won't bite you. Grab his collar!"

Rowdy really is a good dog. He's anything but a sore loser, and he loves meeting new people. Finding himself ensconced between our captors, Rowdy was bright-eyed and waggle-tailed. The men, in contrast, looked stupefied. The damned vampire still hadn't obeyed my order.

"Take his collar," I repeated. As a dog trainer, I believe in giving a command only once, but what choice did I have?

This time, he complied.

Ever mindful of the power of positive reinforcement, I said, "Good! Very good. Now just hang on to him."

Then I turned my attention to Kimi, who still lay outstretched on the rear seat. As I'd suspected, she was gnawing on something. Grasped between her massive front paws was a damp and flattened white carton, the kind used for take-out food. Although Kimi will eat absolutely anything, she shares my fondness for Italian food, especially pizza. The leather seat was smeared with creamy glop that could've been mozzarella, but it was also dusted with white powder. Pizza is harmless. But white powder? Heroin? Cocaine?

"What is my dog eating?" I demanded. "What is this damned powder?"

The men opposite me exchanged glances over Rowdy's bulk.

"Joey," said the vampire, "you left 'em there? Moron." Instead of waiting the millennia it might've taken this remnant of the Ice Age to evolve toward articulate speech, I rummaged in my pockets and found a morsel of home-made liver brownie. "Kimi, trade!" I said brightly. Snatching the soggy carton from her mouth, I kept my part of the bargain by popping in the treat. "Good girl."

Revealed in the soft lights of the limo, Kimi's slimy loot proved to be more or less what I'd surmised, a medium-size piece of thin cardboard, gray on one side, white on the other. Squished and chewed, it was none-theless recognizable as a pastry box. The white powder, then, thank *dog* spelled backward, was nothing more harmful than confectioner's sugar.

"Doughnuts?" I asked.

Stupid me.

To my amazement, it was the Neanderthal, Joey, who replied. "Cannoli."

"Cheese cannoli," I said.

He nodded.

Ricotta cream piped into delectable pasty shells. Well, no wonder Kimi'd leaped. As I've mentioned, she loves Italian food.

Idly smoothing out the dog-moist box, I noticed that the white side bore a name hand-printed in broad felt-tipped black marker. Reading the name, I understood everything.

The name was *Guarini.*

Struggling to believe that Kimi had really done what she'd just done, I said, one ghastly word at a time, "My. Dog. Ate. Enzio. Guarini's. Cannoli." And then as fast as the words could fly out of my mouth, I said, "OhshitsheateGuarini'scannoli."

Roused to Kimi's defense and my own, I sat suddenly upright and pointed at our kidnappers. "The *boss* wants to see me. I get it now. Mr. Guarini wants to see me. And what did the two of you do? You let my dog eat Guarini's cannoli. *You* let it happen. I wasn't doing anything but walking my dogs."

Guarini *was* the boss, you see.

Boss. That's English for capo.

CHAPTER 2

Before I say another word about the Neanderthal and the Transylvanian, and before I introduce Zap the Driver, and especially before I present the boss himself, Enzio Guarini, I want to emphasize that never once in my entire association with the underworld did I see the slightest evidence of anything even remotely like a mobster liberation movement. On the contrary, from Guarini himself all the way down to his lowliest wise guy, the Italian mobsters positively went out of their way to conform to, or even to exceed, the stereotypes in such matters as Town Cars, oversize pinky rings, cannoli consumption, broken noses, the facial expressions of George Raft, and other symbols of racketeer oppression. One exception: They didn't speak with New Jersey accents, but only for reasons of geography, not political consciousness. Boston is Boston. The letter *r* is often silent. *Door* has two syllables: *dough-uh*. That's how they talked. Anyway, in the absence of a Eugene V. Debs type organizer, let me say that the Mafia has nothing to lose but its sinister vehicles, ghastly male jewelry, and gross overreliance on a sexually explicit expletive that begins with *f*. And the world to gain, of course. MOBSTERS OF ALL COUNTRIES, UNITE!

Or preferably, disperse! But that's my biased opinion of what ought to happen, whereas my descriptions of the vehicular, culinary, and personal adornment preferences of Guarini and his underlings are utterly objective and dead accurate, and if you're offended, blame Guarini, not me.

As to the limousine in which Rowdy, Kimi, and I were now incarcerated, I have to admit that far from blaming Guarini for adhering to the stereotype of Mafia transport, I was marveling at the contrast between the splendid, if ill-gotten, conveyance and my battered, if hard-earned, Bronco. To the best of my recollection, the Bronco had once had a suspension system, but the years had unsprung the springs. Rust was eating its body. Belts kept breaking. Dog hair had embedded itself throughout the interior and had, I suspected, migrated forward to clog the engine. Not content with being unreliable and uncomfortable, the Bronco went on to embarrass me by backfiring in public places. The vents blew hot air in the summer and cold in the winter. In these pothole days of spring, the Bronco smashed down into the pits, and when it did, the dogs lurched in their crates, and I got jolted. In brief, I wished that the damned car would vaporize.

The limo, although dated in style, was as silent and smooth as a cat. Its cushioned ride made the roads feel newly paved. The seats were upholstered in real leather. The temperature was neither too hot nor too cold. I'd've bet anything that the turn signals didn't activate the windshield wipers. Geez, maybe the radio even worked. Mine had quit a month ago.

"I take it that we're going to Mr. Guarini's house," I said to his henchmen. "As I recall, his office is in the North End, or at least it used to be, and since we're now in Medford Square, I assume that we're not heading for Hanover Street."

The North End, which is actually east of downtown Boston, is our local Little Italy. Let me hasten to say that I'd been there to eat in Italian restaurants, shop for Italian food, and savor the Old World atmosphere, not to pop in on Enzio Guarini at the notorious "social club," as the newspapers called it, that served as Guarini's headquarters. Medford is north of Boston. Beyond it, near Melrose and Malden, is Munford, where Guarini lived. I wasn't in the habit of dropping in on him there, either. I knew he lived there, because the Boston papers had made a big deal of his recent release from the federal pen and his return to Munford.

"We're heading for Munford, aren't we?" I continued. "I want to know because that's pretty close, and I don't like having my dogs loose in a car. It's not safe. They belong in crates—like the ones you see at the airport. If we have an accident, the dogs could be thrown against the windshield. Or," I added maliciously, "their heads could collide with yours."

As I was about to elaborate, the limo glided into a left turn.

"Munford," I said. "Right?"

The man with the widow's peak nodded. True to stereotype, his nose was a little crooked. His weirdly long fingers were encrusted with heavy rings.

"Thank you." And I smiled, too.

As if fate were responding to the power of positive reinforcement, the limo obediently turned into a driveway. I peered through the tinted glass at a brick colonial that was admittedly big, but otherwise disappointing by comparison with the baronial abodes of Mafia pooh-bahs in movies and on TV. The house had only two noteworthy features. One was the startling absence of the usual suburban rhododendrons or, indeed, any other foundation shrubbery, flower beds, or anything else; the lawn ran right up to the front wall of the house. You know how someone who always wears eyeglasses looks denuded and disoriented without them? That was how Guarini's house looked: naked and confused, as if it were groping around and muttering, "Where on earth did I leave my rhodies?" The second distinctive feature was the blinding illumination cast by industrial floods mounted on the roof and sides of the house and the adjoining two-car garage. Homesick for his former residence, Guarini had nostalgically turned his home into a little prison away from prison. Or maybe he was paranoid. Or smart.

When the engine stopped, I reached over and grabbed

Rowdy's leash while tightening my grip on Kimi's. I knew enough about Guarini to feel confident that the dogs would be welcome. The favor Guarini thought I'd done for him had consisted of helping to close a wholesale dog brokerage operated by his son-in-law, a piece of scum whom Guarini senselessly blamed for the cancer death of Guarini's daughter and justifiably loathed for villainously trafficking in dogs. Although I'd had nothing to do with the death of Guarini's son-in-law, Guarini had nonetheless credited me with it. He'd also applauded my small, if genuine, contribution to animal welfare. So, Guarini loved dogs: If I crossed him, he'd kill me or have me killed, but he'd never hurt Rowdy or Kimi. Just in case I'd somehow offended Guarini, I intended to barricade myself behind my dogs. So what else is new?

Although the limo had stopped, the goons waited for the driver to open the door for them before they clambered out. The dogs and I followed. I guess I could've tried to escape, but I liked my heart the way it was. Beating.

Joey must've noticed that I was a bi t goggle-eyed at the overilluminated barrenness of the place. "So's no one can't hide nowhere," he told me.

Before I'd finished sorting out the negatives, the driver distracted me by commenting on Rowdy and Kimi, albeit in an obnoxious way. "Tough," he said with approval. The driver himself looked anything but tough: He was scrawny and pasty faced, with a dissipated air that made his age hard to estimate. I settled on a guess of twenty-two, but an aged twenty-two. His short brown hair was barbered, as opposed to styled, and perhaps in imitation of old-time-movie thugs, he wore a trench coat belted tightly around his skinny middle. Pointing a stubby finger at Kimi, he said, "How much you want for him?"

"Her. She's not for sale."

The attraction was understandable. Kimi's facial markings make her look tough. Her "full mask," as it's called, the combination of a black cap, eye goggles, and a bar down the nose, creates a banditlike appearance. In contrast, Rowdy's all-white countenance, an "open face," suggests candidness and honesty. Both dogs, however, have soft, dark eyes and warm, gentle expressions, and neither Rowdy nor Kimi is in the least bit deceitful, by which I mean that instead of sneaking around waiting until your back is turned, these dogs will snatch food off your plate and otherwise brazenly do what they're going to do right before your very eyes.

As the driver was beginning to make an offer on Rowdy, the vampire cut him off by saying, "Zap, shut up."

"Hey, Al, I was only asking," Zap whined.

"Don't ask, you moron. Just shut up." Al blew his nose.

Al and Joey headed across the lawn toward the front door. As soon as their backs were turned, Zap muttered, "Shut up yourself, ya friggin' vampire." I later learned that the Boston newspapers referred to Al Favuzza in the same way: *Alphonse "The Count" Favuzza,* typically preceded by a phrase such as *alleged Mob associate.*

Let me not linger over Mob monikers because I'm dying . . . well, poor choice of expression. Let's start over.

I'm eager to introduce you to Enzio Guarini. A few minutes after Zap the Driver had tried to buy Kimi, and a minute or two after an elephantine man had admitted us to the house, the dogs and I, accompanied by Al and Joey, were waiting for Enzio Guarini in what had obviously been his late wife's living room. True to stereotype, the room had numerous table lamps in the form of half-naked Greco-Roman goddesses. The rug, in shades of red and blue, depicted fully togaed people loitering in front of a pillared temple. The walls were thick with large oil paintings devoted to two contrasting subjects, first, Italy—canals, gondolas, ruins—and, second, Norway, but only as it pertained to Norwegian elkhounds—a forest scene with a pack of dogs staring at a moose, a sentimental portrait of a rustic cabin near the door of which stood two elkhounds and a man in serious need of a shampoo.

On the otherwise empty surface of a mile-long desk lay a copy of the latest issue of *Dog's Life* magazine folded open to an article I'd written about pet mummification. The illustration caught Al "The Count" Favuzza's eye just as I'd hoped it would catch every reader's eye when I'd done it on my computer. It showed a human-shaped Egyptian mummy, wrappings and all, but I'd tinkered with the portrait panel by replacing the drawing of a man's face with a close-up of Rowdy's head. Favuzza stared at the illustration, then studied Rowdy, then said, "Hey, that looks just like him."

"It is," I said. "I wrote the article. And I put that picture together on my computer."

"Trick photography," Favuzza said. "This some kind of a joke?"

"The picture? Yeah, sort of."

"Turning your dog into a mummy."

"People do it," I said. "That's what the article's about. It's expensive. But some people can't stand the idea of burial. Or cremation. So they have their dogs mummified. Or their cats. Or for that matter, themselves. The same company does human mummies. Or it's going to. The people who've signed up are all still alive."

"Does it work?"

"I think so. I mean, the mummies from ancient Egypt are in pretty good shape, and they're thousands of years old. So if you want your body preserved, or your dog's or your cat's, then yes, it works. The process is pretty complicated. Preservatives, chemicals, all kinds of stuff. Maybe you should read my article. It's mostly about dogs, but the principle is exactly the same."

As Favuzza and I were holding this grisly discussion, Rowdy and Kimi snuffled around within the limits of their six-foot leashes. Then a door burst open, and in strode Enzio Guarini. For a moment, I mistook the aura he radiated for mere vitality. My wise dogs weren't fooled. Recognizing raw power for what it was, they fell to the floor at Guarini's feet. Even now, I must remind myself that if Guarini's body had been animated by a spirit milder than his, the physical Guarini, so to speak, would've been unremarkable: a man of seventy, neither short nor tall, with gray hair and brown eyes, an ordinary man who carried an ebony cane. Considering who Guarini was, it should, I suppose, have been crooked. In fact, it was a straight walking stick with a brass grip.

Part of Guarini's considerable charm lay in the warmth of his smile. He beamed at me. Then, with the aid of the cane, he bent to greet Rowdy and Kimi, to whose exposed underbellies he delivered thumps and scratches. As Guarini began to rise, Joey leaned toward him without actually stepping to his aid, probably because Guarini had arrived with yet two more men. These two, a matched pair, were at least six three, with broad shoulders, bullet-shaped heads, and small, dead eyes. The bodyguards, as they obviously were, wore white shirts and mud-colored sport coats. Dog person that he was, Guarini had on a gray sweatshirt embellished with the head of a Norwegian elkhound, a breed to which I am partial. The elkhound is a moose-hunting breed, not a sled dog. Nonetheless, elkhounds look quite a bit like small gray malamutes with curly tails.

Having won me over big by welcoming Rowdy and Kimi, Guarini, now standing upright, extended his right hand and, still smiling that killer smile, said, "Miss Holly Winter. I am delighted. Thank you for accepting the invitation of a loyal fan."

"The pleasure is mine," I said. The boss's handshake was strong. Mine was stronger. I've spent my whole life with big dogs. I groom Rowdy and Kimi myself. I've got wrists of dog-tempered steel.

"You've met my associates," Guarini said. "Al Favuzza." He gestured to the Count. "And Joey Cortiniglia." The Neanderthal.

My kidnappers nodded. Neither smiled. As I somehow expected, Guarini didn't go on to introduce the bodyguards; then and afterward, he treated them simply as mobile defense systems.

In that sense, he was no hypocrite.

Turning to Favuzza and Joey, Guarini said, to my alarm, "Me and Miss Winter got private business here." *This ain't personal. It's business.* I'd heard that line in a hundred Mafia movies. It's what the hit man says just before he pulls the trigger. To my amazement, however, no one shot me. All that happened was that Al Favuzza and Joey Cortiniglia left the room. The bodyguards stayed. At Guarini's invitation, I took a seat in a big armchair slipcovered in a boldly flowered fabric. He remained standing.

"I have a problem," he began.

Despite his overt friendliness, my heart pounded.

"With a dog," he continued. "A puppy."

My sigh of relief must have been audible.

"I've been away," he said.

I kept a straight face.

"On my return, I bought the puppy."

"An elkhound." Years ago, he'd owned two champions.

"My breed." He lifted his right hand briefly to his heart, thus patting the dog depicted on his sweatshirt. "I bought him from Irene Izakson."

I nodded. "If I were looking for an elkhound myself, she's the first person I'd call." True. Like everyone else who's anyone in dogs—everyone over a certain age, that is—Irene was a friend of that legendary grande dame of the Dog Fancy, Marissa Winter, my late mother. "How old is the puppy?"

"Four months. A male. Frey."

Norse god of peace and prosperity. It's a popular malamute name, too. In fact, it's a popular dog name.

I looked straight into Guarini's eyes and smiled knowingly. "But a little less peaceful than you counted on."

Guarini slowly shook his head back and forth. With a self-deprecating smile, he raised a hand and knocked himself lightly on the head.

"It happens all the time," I assured him "Puppy energy. People forget what it's like. Everyone does. We love our old dogs. They die. What we remember are our *old* dogs." I paused. "Let me guess. Frey jumps on you. And on other people. He doesn't come when he's called. He's noisy? The more you tell him not to bark, the more he does. He chews furniture." I wasn't guessing. The legs of the mile-long desk bore fresh tooth marks. My next observation wasn't a guess, either; the hideous rug camouflaged the stains, but it didn't entirely hide them. "He has accidents in the house."

Guarini reached into the right pocket of his pants. I naturally assumed that he was going to pull out a gun and shoot me for insulting his dog. In fact, he produced a bright blue cotton leash, or what had recently been one, anyway. Looking chagrined, he held it up to display the fine job that Frey had done of reducing it to macramé.

"Very artistic," I said.

Guarini laughed. Then he licked his lips, hunched one shoulder, looked at the ceiling, and finally rested his gaze on Rowdy and Kimi, who were politely lying on the rug enjoying the interesting scent.

"I see," I said. "He's growling at you. Irene's lines have good temperaments. Outstanding temperaments. If he's growling when you get near his food bowl, he can learn not to do it. If he growls when you try to take his toys, he can learn to give them to you." Motivated by fear, professional pride, and, I admit, curiosity, I went on. "I can fix all of it. I can teach Frey to walk nicely on leash. To stop jumping. I can help you teach him to be a good dog."

"That's why I invited you here," said Guarini.

Thus began my new career: Holly Winter, dog trainer to the Mob.

CHAPTER 3

Over the next two weeks, I repeatedly informed Enzio Guarini that violence begets violence. "With this puppy," I kept saying, "we're using gentle modern methods." Indeed, I fervently preached the gospel of positive reinforcement to a Mob boss who was reputed to have murdered so many people that he himself had probably lost count long ago.

I translated my faith into works by training Guarini's charming elkhound puppy, Frey, sometimes at Guarini's house, sometimes at mine. When Frey was delivered to me in Cambridge, Zap drove him in the limousine, and when I went to Munford, Zap chauffeured me there. During those first two weeks, I continued to feel the fear, curiosity, and professional pride that had made me practically volunteer to help Guarini with Frey. A few times when I was sitting at home in my cozy kitchen in the company of no one but my dogs, I admitted to myself that I also felt titillated to play a small and blameless role in the life of so notorious a figure as Enzio Guarini. I was flattered by Guarini's esteem for me; in an unpardonably callous way, I was starstruck.

Guarini and I spoke regularly on the phone, and Frey was now housebroken, but until the evening I'm about to describe, Guarini had managed to avoid almost every training session. The results were predictable. When Frey and I worked alone together, the puppy was absolutely terrific. According to Guarini, however, the puppy wouldn't listen to a word he said. Furthermore, because Guarini had forbidden me to take Frey out in public, the puppy had no experience with ordinary sights, scents, and sounds. It's a tribute to my love of dogs and my fear of Guarini that I'd dared to argue with the boss. In one of our phone consultations, I'd said, "Yes, there's a slight health risk in taking him places, but it's also risky to keep him isolated from the real world. The last time Frey was here, when I was taking him back to your car, some-one rode by on a bicycle, and he was startled and scared. He needs to get used to bicycles and kids and crowds and so on. And I'm warning you. If I keep training him with food and you don't, he's going to watch me and obey me, and there's nothing I can do to stop that except tell you what you already know, which is that if you want Frey to be *your* dog, you need to train him, too."

Guarini's first response had been to ask who was riding the bicycle.

"Some woman," I'd said. "Cambridge type. She's irrelevant. The point is that Frey needs to get used to bicycles and strangers and everything else. He needs socialization."

It's a tribute to Guarini's love of dogs that he listened to me at all. He rejected my advice that he take Frey to puppy kindergarten class. Offering no explanation, he refused to let me take Frey myself. Guarini did, however, submit to my badgering by agreeing to meet me where we were now, behind the mall at the Fresh Pond rotary in Cambridge. After Guarini and I had gone back and forth about locations, we'd settled on the area between Danehy Park and the rear of the mall, just behind Loaves and Fishes, which would be easy to mistake for a natural-foods supermarket, but is actually a religious institution whose followers subscribe to the belief that they'll be poisoned if they eat anything from an ordinary supermarket. Danehy Park, in contrast, is no temple of purity. It used to be a dump. It still has no mature trees. The mall is surrounded by blacktop, and the main parking lot is in front of the stores. There was nothing along the side of the building except a laundromat. The openness of the spot was probably why Guarini had agreed to it. You may recall that in remarking on the absence of foundation plantings at Guarini's house, Joey Cortiniglia had said, "So's no one can't hide nowhere." Well, no one couldn't hide nowhere here, either.

Although the Loaves and Fishes mall and the park are an easy walk from my house, I'd used my car so I could take Rowdy and Kimi for a walk in the park and then have a safe place to stash them while I worked with Guarini and Frey. Just as planned, when the dogs and I returned to the Bronco, Guarini was arriving with what struck me as a small army and probably was one in the literal sense of being a company of armed men. The two bodyguards towered over Guarini, who wore a tweed coat and one of those stupid-looking tweed hats. The hat was anything but cool, but the ebony cane more than compensated. As a dog trainer rather than a connoisseur of cool, I was happy to note that the coat, probably chosen to disguise dog hair, had capacious pockets well suited to hold the cheese, meat, and other dog treats I'd instructed Guarini to have with him. Zap the Driver had parked the limo between my decrepit Bronco and a shiny new silver Chevy Suburban. Lounging near the Texas Cadillac were Joey "The Neanderthal" Cortiniglia, as I thought of him, and Al "The Count" Favuzza, as the Boston papers and maybe even his friends referred to him. Everyone except Guarini wore what I came to think of as the Mob uniform: a zip-front nylon or cotton warm-up jacket in a solid, neutral color, trousers rather than jeans, and running shoes or loafers. The surprising and invariant feature of the uniform was that with the exception of an occasional pair of running shoes, every single piece of clothing worn by everyone but Guarini looked cheap.

In retrospect, it seems to me that Joey Cortiniglia acted nervous. I can't be sure. He and Favuzza kept looking around, but so did Zap and the bodyguards. Maybe all of them were just doing their job, which was, at the moment, to protect Guarini. Still, I have the vivid impression that Joey fidgeted and that his face was damp.

I greeted Guarini, Zap, Jocy, and Favuzza just as if they were normal human beings instead of organized-crime figures. Rowdy and Kimi outdid me by wagging their beautiful tails and sounding peals of *woo-woo-woo*, but they directed their salutation exclusively to the alpha figure, Guarini, and disregarded the lesser-ranking members of his pack. The only ones I ignored were the bodyguards.

"Where's Frey?" I asked.

Zap jabbed a thumb at the limo.

"Let me just crate Rowdy and Kimi," I said to Guarini, "and then we'll get to work."

As I was opening the Bronco's door, however, Joey offered to take care of the dogs so they wouldn't have to be, as he phrased it, "locked up." As he went on to explain, "Them dogs didn't do nothing wrong."

Mindful that Guarini had recently been released from a federal pen and that the topic of incarceration was doubtless a sensitive one for Joey, too, I was inclined to accept his offer. After exchanging glances with Guarini and getting his nod of approval, I said to Joey, "Okay, but no matter what happens, hang on to their leashes. Don't let go! And you'd better keep them away from other dogs. They're usually all right, but if someone's five-pound lap dog decides to tackle them, they won't back down, so if you see another dog, walk in the opposite direction. Or put them in the car. I'll leave it unlocked."

A glimmer of something weirdly reminiscent of intelligence crossed Joey's face. "My wife's got a little tiny dog," he said.

"They're often very bright," I remarked truthfully. "Very trainable."

"Not this one," Joey said. "Not Anthony."

Favuzza snorted. Or maybe he intended to laugh. The sound was throaty and repulsive.

"Be that as it may," I said breezily, "don't let my dogs get loose. We won't be long. Frey is just a puppy, so we're only going to do a short session. We'll be in front of Loaves and Fishes or right around the corner at the end of the mall, so if you need any help with my dogs, just holler for me." To Rowdy and Kimi, I delivered my usual farewell. "Be good dogs. I'll be right back."

After I finished giving my orders, it was Guarini's turn. Joey—and by implication, Rowdy and Kimi—were to stay right near where all of us were now. Favuzza was to patrol on foot; Guarini made an arc with his arm. Having finally retrieved Frey from the limo, Guarini told Zap to get in and drive around. These instructions struck me as vague, but the men seemed to understand. The body-guards required no instructions; they were apparently on permanent orders to cover Guarini.

As to Frey, let me quote one of the most oft-quoted statements ever made about the virtues of dogs, namely, "The more I get to know men, the more I find myself loving dogs." Those words are Charles de Gaulle's, but he was quoting someone else. Anyway, in contrast to the vampirish Favuzza, the barely hominid Joey, the jaded Zap, the robotic bodyguards, and the deadly, although charming, Guarini, the elkhound puppy was a beautiful little gray fur ball of lovable, exuberant innocence. Imagine a wind-up toy in the form of a gray bear. Around Frey's neck was a little red puppy collar. Attached to it was a six-foot red cotton leash that at the moment served as the target of Frey's considerable energy. With a naughty glance at Guarini, the puppy grabbed the leash in his teeth, growled softly, and shook his pretend prey with the obvious intention of breaking its neck. From the human end of the leash, Guarini said, "Stop that! Frey, no! No, Frey! Bad dog!"

"When we speak to Frey," I said, "we are reinforcing his behavior. If we say his name, we are providing especially powerful positive reinforcement."

Royal *we*.

At the sound of my voice, Frey quit the game. Bright puppy that he was, he knew that I had better games in mind.

"Frey, sit!" He sat. Instantly, I used my clicker and followed the sound with a treat, specifically, with one of the morsels of liver brownie that remained in my pocket. Smiling at the puppy, I stated the obvious, namely, that positive reinforcement works. Then I delivered the line about violence begetting violence and my pitch for gentle methods. "You brought the clicker I left at your house for you? And treats?"

We were now next to the building, between the laundromat and the liquor store that's next to Loaves and Fishes. If Guarini had forgotten to bring food, we could get some right around the corner. Same old same old!

Dogs are easy to train: Provide positive reinforcement for the behavior you want and only for the behavior you want. What is positive reinforcement? Anything the dog likes. Result: good dog. But people? Damn!

Guarini did, however, produce a clicker and a few pieces of puppy chow.

"That's good that you have the clicker," I said. Positive reinforcement for the behavior you want, right?

"The nuns used to use these things," Guarini complained, "and not for positive reinforcement."

"We're not nuns. And you don't have to use the clicker. The clicker is an event marker. It tells Frey exactly what we like. But you can just use food and praise. Just remember to give the food and the praise *after* Frey does what you want, not before. We're not using food as a lure. A lure comes *before* the behavior." Translating the distinction into my pupil's own language, I said, "In other words, we're not bribing him. We're paying him off. But if we want the payoff to work, it has to be a really good payoff. Meat. Cheese." Examining the kibble Guarini had shown me, I said, "This stuff isn't going to get us the results we want." As we strolled toward the front of the mall, I continued. "What we've got here are one-dollar bills. What we need are twenties. At least." We'd now reached the liquor store at the corner of the mall. "But ones are better than nothing," I said. "I'm going to run into Loaves and Fishes and get some cheese and beef. I'll be right back. In the meantime, stay here and work with Frey. If he watches your face, click and treat. Or if someone goes by here with a shopping cart,

and he's calm, click and treat." After muttering the slogan
of this school of dog training ("Catch him doing something right!"), I dashed into Loaves and Fishes, made my
way past the worshipers genuflecting in the aisles to read
labels, and after waiting a while at the deli counter and
then again at the checkout, bought a quarter-pound each
of roast beef and sliced provolone. My own dogs prefer
cheddar, but in case I haven't mentioned it lately, let me
remind you that Frey was growing up in an Italian family,
hence the provolone.

When I emerged from the store, Guarini, flanked by
the bodyguards, was just where I'd left him. (Good capo!)
Frey had his eyes on his master, and Guarini was not only
clicking and treating, but smiling and saying, "Good
dog!" Except to hand Guarini some beef, I didn't inter-
fere. Let me mention that it never crossed my mind that
Guarini might have moved during my absence. Let me
also note, however, that I'd been fooled more than once
during the Open obedience group exercises when I'd left
Rowdy on an apparently solid sit, marched out of sight
with the other handlers, and returned to find him in the
identical position—only to be told by the smirking judge
that the spectators had gotten a big kick out of watching
Rowdy break position, step forward, roll onto his back,
wave his big paws in the air, return to the exact spot
where I'd left him, and sit where I'd authoritatively commanded him to stay. Guarini's eyes lacked the telltale
gleam I'd come to recognize in Rowdy's; absolutely nothing made me wonder whether Guarini might have budged.
In any case, training Guarini to train his puppy imme-

diately occupied all my attention, and now that Guarini was offering beef and cheese, the training held Frey's rapt attention, too. I now realize that the dapper Guarini with his ebony walking stick, his noisy clicker, his adorable puppy, and his massive bodyguards must have been memorable. Had anyone—the police, for instance—sought witnesses to testify to Guarini's presence, the task would've been easy. At the time, ignoring the occasional shopper who lingered to admire Frey, I concentrated on nodding approval to Guarini as he doled out clicks and treats.

I'd said that the training session would be short. It was. Perhaps ten minutes elapsed from the moment I left Loaves and Fishes to the moment I announced that Frey had had enough. How long had it taken me to buy the beef and cheese? Ten minutes? I'd had to wait at the deli counter, and there'd been people ahead of me in the checkout line. Adding on the time it had taken to walk from the cars to the front of the mall, the total time since I'd left Joey Cortiniglia with my dogs was, say, twenty-five or thirty minutes. For the record, let me note that not once had I peered around the corner of the building to check on Rowdy and Kimi. I'd been busy. Besides, Joey Cortiniglia wasn't big on brains, but he was brawny enough to hang on to two malamutes. Let me also mention that I hadn't glimpsed the limo or Al Favuzza since we'd left them. Finally, the only people I saw who looked like mobsters were my own companions.

So, maybe thirty minutes after I'd left Rowdy and Kimi with Joey, when the training session was over,

Guarini, Frey, the bodyguards, and I rounded the corner of the mall at the liquor store. "Now," I was saying, "if Frey is about to jump on you or someone else, you tell him, 'Frey, sit,' and when he does, click and . . . WHERE THE HELL ARE MY DOGS?"

CHAPTER 4

Even before I'd finished shouting, the bodyguards had formed a human barricade around Guarini. They sensed danger; their response was correct. My own first—and, I should note, incorrect—response was anger at Joey. My second was guilt. Rowdy and Kimi were the better half of myself. Why had I entrusted them to a Neanderthal, even a Neanderthal who worked for Enzio Guarini?

Joey Cortiniglia was nowhere in sight. My Bronco and the silver Suburban were where we'd left them, facing away from us, my Bronco on the right, the Texas Cadillac on the left. The limo, which had been parked between the cars, was gone, as it was supposed to be; Guarini had told Zap to cruise around. Al Favuzza, who'd been assigned to foot patrol, was nowhere to be seen. Believe me, I looked, not for Favuzza, of course, but for my dogs.

Joey, the big dope, must've decided to take them for a walk. He'd probably decided to let them make friends with some miniature canine fiend that they were now disemboweling. Damn it! Joey knew that my car was unlocked. If anything had happened, he should've put the dogs in the car.

Maybe he had. I pounded across the blacktop. The bodyguards made no effort to stop me. They were, after all, Guarini's guards and not mine. Guarini could've called out a warning to me. He didn't. I might not have heeded it, anyway. I made directly for the Bronco and was running so fast when I reached it that I slammed my open palms against the rear window while simultaneously peering in at the dogs' empty crates. If Rowdy had been loose in the car, he'd have put himself where, in his opinion, he naturally belonged in life as well as in vehicles: in the driver's seat. But the entire damned car was filled with the absence of dogs.

Listening for the distant, dreaded roar of a dog fight, I was startled when a low-pitched grinding noise drew my gaze to the passenger-side front bumper. Sticking out from under the car was a softly wagging malamute tail. I traced it to the rest of Kimi's body. The grinding emanated from her jaws and from Rowdy's. Kimi's tail, the one I'd spotted first, was executing a lackadaisical wave instead of a vigorous thump because she was concentrating most of her energy on gnawing the hunk of bone she held between her forepaws. Still safely attached to her collar, her leather leash had been looped around a thick section of the undercarriage and snapped to her collar.

Rowdy was identically hitched to the other side of the
car. He, too, was occupied in chewing a large, fresh-
looking bone. My dogs live a deprived life; they almost
never get bones. Malamutes have tremendously powerful
jaws. I'm always afraid that even comparatively safe bones
like frozen raw knucklebones will break or splinter and
that what's intended to be a dog's treat will result in
intestinal surgery and a stay in a critical care unit.

I stooped down near Rowdy and was about to ask him
what the hell was going on when I finally noticed Joey
Cortiniglia. And the gore. Joey's caveman body was
stretched out lengthwise just under the silver Suburban,
feet toward the front of the big car. He lay on his back
with his right arm visible—and visibly limp. Death
hadn't softened the prognathous thrust of his jaw. He'd
been shot in the head. I have a strong stomach. I've
whelped puppies, cleaned deep wounds, and mopped up
reeking canine messes of every sort—liquid, semiformed,
and solid. Enough said, except that I found myself sitting
on the blacktop feeling not only queasy but disoriented,
as if the dogs and I were trapped in a surrealist painting
entitled *Gangland Slaying with Woman and Malamutes*. For
a moment, I imagined that the bones Rowdy and Kimi
were chewing had come from human legs.

The next thing I knew, Enzio Guarini was talking to
me. He informed me that I wasn't here. "You tie up the
dogs like that?"

"Of course not. And I don't give them bones. Malamutes—"

Guarini interrupted. In a gentle voice that commanded

obedience, he said very slowly, "Take them and go home. This didn't happen."

By now, Favuzza was on the scene, Zap and the limo had returned, and two more men had appeared, gigantic twins so gargantuan and so identical that I had to wonder whether I was hallucinating double. As I followed orders by undoing the hard knots in the leather leads, unhitching the dogs, and putting them in their crates in the car, Guarini's men went about the gruesome task of encasing Joey's body in heavy green trash bags and loading it into the Suburban. The bodyguards, as always, remained silent. Zap, Favuzza, and the monstrous twins didn't exactly whistle while they worked, but they did talk, and although I avoided the area between my Bronco and the Suburban, snatches of conversation reached me. Favuzza made his adenoidal snorting noise. "Blackie wouldn't've hurt a dog. Somebody else would've shot them. And giving them bones is Blackie all over." He then asked Zap a question I didn't hear, and Zap replied that he'd looked everywhere. Out of the corner of my eye, I saw the twins raise Joey's body. After that, they seemed to concentrate on searching the Suburban. I heard one of them report to Guarini: "Nothing."

"Blackie must've been running low on cash," Favuzza said.

"Don't take nothing for granted," Guarini said. "You get me a name. You got that? Could've been Blackie. Could've been someone else. This is a message to me, and I want to know who the fuck sent it. Get me that name."

When I'd finally transferred both dogs to my Bronco,

I did exactly what Guarini had ordered. I got into my car and drove home. When I got there, instead of going next door to ring Lieutenant Kevin Dennehy's bell, I led Rowdy and Kimi directly to our own house. Once inside, I thought about calling Kevin. I didn't do it. In one respect, I did, however, disobey Enzio Guarini: I remembered what had happened; I did not forget the sight of Joey Cortiniglia's body. I told myself that my mind, at least, was free.

CHAPTER 5

Sex and death. About a hundred and thirty-three days before Joey Cortiniglia took a fatal bullet in the brain, Rowdy had reveled in the delusion that he'd died and gone to heaven, which is to say that he'd been bred to CH Jazzland's Embraceable You. Emma, as she was called, had flown from the state of Washington for the carefully planned tryst. In case you are unfamiliar with the reproductive rites of the Exalted Order of the Pure-bred Pooch, I should mention that creating new lives from Rowdy and Emma had undoubtedly involved more forethought than had gone into eradicating life from Joey Cortiniglia. Here in dogs, the breeder of a litter is the owner of the bitch—a technical term, not a slur, and certainly not a derogation of Emma, who even before finishing her championship had gone Reserve Winners

Bitch—technical term, see?—at the Alaskan Malamute National Specialty, an honor roughly translatable from dogspeak to Standard English as Next to the Top Female Who Hasn't Finished Her Championship as Judged at the Annual Ritual Gathering of Persons Infatuated with Alaskan Malamutes. In other words, Emma had been singled out as excellent against heavy national competition. Furthermore, after finishing, she'd won an Award of Merit at the National, too.

Rowdy, too, had finished his championship and had acquired an impressive list of titles after his name for achievements in . . . well, if I start on Rowdy, I'll never get back to Joey Cortiniglia. Emma's owner, Cindy Neely, and I had exchanged and pored over pedigrees and health information. Emma and Rowdy were free of hip dysplasia, eye disease, hypothyroidism, and other afflictions. As to safe sex, neither was infected with brucellosis. Temperament? Each was as sweet as the other. My own Kimi, I might mention, had a streak of single-minded intensity that in my opinion made her an iffy candidate for breeding. The trait suited me perfectly. I adored Kimi for it. I drew on her strength. But she was just too much dog for most people, even for most malamute people. So, I didn't want to breed her.

As to Joey's murder, what forethought had gone into that? Any? Grab a gun. Pull the trigger. Well, a bit more. Joey's killer had also been armed with bones for my dogs. Big deal.

One final point of comparison. Cindy Neely and I had signed a stud contract that spelled out the terms of the

breeding. Had Joey's killer also had a contract? My contract had given me a choice of a stud fee for Rowdy's
services or a puppy in lieu of cash. I'd wanted a puppy.
But Rowdy, Kimi, Tracker, and I live on the first floor
of my three-story house. The bank and I own the place,
and without the rents from the two apartments, the bank
would soon own the whole thing. The yard is fenced, but
it's small; near Harvard Square, I'm lucky to have a yard
at all. It would be impossible for me to toss a third malamute into my existing pack because Rowdy wouldn't
accept another male, and Kimi wouldn't tolerate another
female. I had no room for an outdoor kennel. Still, having
to settle for a stud fee almost broke my heart.

But I was rescued by sex and death, or at least by sex-
gone-by and the death of . . . well, maybe I'd better explain. Early that past autumn, the man in my life and
the vet in Rowdy's and Kimi's lives, Steve Delaney, had
done the unthinkable by getting married. Not to me, I
should add. Steve had asked me first. Second. Third. . . .
I'd refused. Why? In retrospect, I think that the true
answer is that it never occurred to me that he'd marry
someone else. It certainly never occurred to me that Steve,
the most honest, ethical person in the world, would marry
a crook. Specifically, an embezzler. But that's a whole
other story. He was now getting divorced. And that's yet
another story. What's relevant to this one, besides Steve's
upright character and touchiness about violations of the
law, is that totally out of the blue—actually, totally out
of the wolf gray and white—when he and I hadn't spoken
for months, he called to say that he was interested in a

malamute puppy and had heard that Rowdy had been bred. Even if Steve had been a stranger, I'd have thought it was an excellent idea to replace his horrible about-to-be ex-wife with a wonderful dog. As it was, Steve was anything but a stranger, and he wasn't proposing to replace the dreadful Anita with any old fantastic dog of any old splendid breed, either, but with a puppy of *my* breed sired by *my* dog. So, sex: Rowdy and Emma's, death: the demise of Steve's marriage.

Careful breeder that she was, Cindy interviewed Steve at great length to make sure he was good enough to own one of Emma's puppies, and let me just mention as a little aside that if Steve had been half as thorough about screening a wife as Cindy was about screening a puppy buyer . . . well, let me not add that after all, but jump to Logan Airport, where Steve and I arrived at eight o'clock in the evening on the day after Joey Cortiniglia's murder. We were at Logan to meet the plane carrying Rowdy's son, Emma's son, Cindy's puppy, Steve's puppy, and therefore almost my puppy. The plane wasn't due until 9:14. We were early because a certain impatient person was exuberantly excited at the prospect of getting her hands on Rowdy's, Emma's, Cindy's, and Steve's puppy. Since we were going to pick him up at the passenger baggage claim, we weren't stuck waiting way out in the cargo area, which lacked the amenity of passionate interest to anyone genetically predisposed to develop malamute fever, namely, restaurants.

After checking the arrivals monitor, Steve said, "On time. You hungry?"

"I'm half malamute," I said. Then I wondered whether it had somehow been the wrong thing to say. Maybe I should just have said yes. Or lied and said no.

Steve didn't seem to object. On the contrary, he said, "I'm joining the clan myself in an hour and fifteen minutes." His voice was as deep and rumbly as ever, and in most ways, he looked the same as always, tall and sinewy, with incredible blue-green eyes. His hair was wavy and brown, and was looking like itself again now that he'd had it professionally clipped by one of his vet techs rather than by a Newbury Street stylist chosen by his almost ex-wife. I'd've bet that Anita had picked out the wool turtleneck he was wearing. Its sleeves had an odd shape that somehow looked expensively trendy, but I felt confident that he was wearing it now only because of its color, which was dark wolf gray.

I pointed to a nearby cafeteria and said, "Is this okay?" The appealing alternative was the airport branch of a chain of seafood restaurants. A year ago, it would have gone without saying that we'd have a civilized meal instead of loading up two oily-feeling trays and then gobbling burgers and fries; in those days, we'd both have assumed that Steve would pay the bill. He had a successful veterinary practice in Cambridge, whereas my career in dog writing, otherwise known as my Noble Sacrifice to the Arts, left me chronically broke, in part, of course, because most of the pittance I earned went literally and immediately to the dogs.

"Madame," said Steve, "in celebration of the arrival of Jazzland's As Time Goes By, please do me the honor of

accepting my humble invitation." He swept his arm fish-
ward, so to speak. *Jazzland* was Cindy's kennel name. The
puppy was to be called Sammy.

So, we ended up in the seafood restaurant at a table for
two near the bar. Mounted above the bar was a big televison with the volume turned blessedly low. At this
point, we weren't watching television, but studying our
menus. It was taking me an atypically long time to decide
what to order, especially considering that there was lobster on the menu and someone else was paying. The hitch
was that I'd first met Steve's wife at a clambake that had
included lobster. Steve had been there, and I was now
afraid of reviving best-forgotten memories. On the other
hand, my *not* ordering lobster might remind him of that
occasion, too. The pasta dishes and the steamed mussels
had delectable-sounding Italian names, but I was so determined to keep Steve ignorant of my relationship with
Enzio Guarini that I wanted to avoid even the most
oblique reference to Italy. Pondering the haddock, sword-
fish, and halibut, I kept thinking of that famous line from
The Godfather about Luca Brasi, a ridiculous association,
I admit, since it's obviously possible to request and de-
vour vertebrate sea creatures without so much as hinting
at underworld figures who sleep with the fishes.

"Fried oysters," I finally said, and then suddenly realized, to my horror, that oysters were a legendary aphro-
disiac.

Happily, what I'd overlooked throughout all this obsess-
ing was Steve's entirely scientific, completely unpsychol-
ogical mind-set. Without a trace of self-consciousness, he

chose fish chowder followed by finnan haddie, and per-
suaded me to get the fried oysters as an appetizer, followed
by a baked stuffed lobster.

"Wine?" he asked.

Out of the corner of my eye, I was aghast to spot an
all-too-familiar young man taking a seat on a bar stool.
What was Guarini's driver, Zap, *doing* here?

"Nothing Italian!" I blurted out.

Naturally, Steve was startled. "You have something
against Italy all of a sudden?"

"No, not at all. I'm just not in a mood for . . . never
mind. I'd like a glass of white wine."

Relieved to have uttered a few words without wifely
or gangland associations, I managed to get through the
ordering of food and drink in moderate comfort. I
couldn't help sneaking in glances at Zap, but Steve didn't
seem to notice. Indeed, it occurred to me that one of
Steve's many virtues was a relaxing tendency not to scru-
tinize everything I did. Also, since we'd been seeing very
little of each other, we had plenty of catching up to do.
Over drinks and appetizers, we talked about friends and
about Rowdy and Kimi and about Lady, his pointer, and
India, his shepherd, and neither of us said a word about
disbarred lawyer ex-wives-to-be, Italy, or racketeers. Zap
continued to sit alone at the bar and gave no sign of
noticing my presence. All went well until just as Steve's
finnan haddie and my lobster were served, the bartender
turned up the volume on the television, and onto the
screen flashed a photo of Blackie Lanigan with the super-
imposed caption "Where's Blackie?"

In turning our attention to the televison, Steve and I were no different from everyone else in its range, and the smile that crossed Steve's face was just a particularly attractive version of those that appeared on the faces of the entire population of Greater Boston whenever this famous question was asked. In Boston, *everyone* recognized Blackie Lanigan's picture and loved wondering where he was. Why? Because Blackie headed the FBI's list of Ten Most Wanted Fugitives, and Blackie was a Boston crook. Around here, it's not every day that a local boy makes bad. My buddy Kevin Dennehy took a particular interest in Blackie because their backgrounds were somewhat similar. Although Kevin had grown up in Cambridge and was part Italian, he liked to claim that he and Blackie were both Boston Irish and had had the same occupational choices: cop, robber, or priest. In espousing this bigoted view, Kevin always wore a wry expression. His eyes glimmered. Cop that he was, he rationalized his Blackie mania as professional duty. Still, I felt convinced that Kevin the Cop saw Blackie the Crook as the shadow side of himself, or, as Kevin phrased it, "there but for fortune." Anyway, everyone in Boston who read the papers or the local magazines or who watched televison or listened to the radio or just hung around with other people knew all about Blackie Lanigan, but I knew even more than most other people because of listening to Kevin Dennehy.

"No one ever gets tired of it," Steve remarked without moving his eyes from the monitor. "Here's a guy who's been on the lam for . . . what is it? Five years? And there hasn't been any real news about him in all that time, but, hey, it's Boston, so Blackie's permanent news."

The narrator of this latest Blackie TV special was now reading the list of crimes for which Blackie was wanted by the FBI: racketeering influenced and corrupt organizations—RICO—eighteen counts of murder, conspiracy to commit murder, conspiracy to commit extortion, money laundering, narcotics distribution, and so on. If it was bad, Blackie had either done it or conspired to do it or both, and the FBI wanted him for all these deeds and conspiracies. Just how eager was the FBI to catch Blackie? The reward for information leading directly to his arrest was a million dollars.

"I hope you're remembering to keep your eyes out for Blackie," I said to Steve, "because he loves animals, you know. You can never tell when he might show up in your waiting room."

Steve laughed.

"I'm serious. Kevin knows everything about Blackie, and he's always talking about him, and he says that Blackie is crazy about dogs." The television displayed one of the close-ups of Blackie that the local papers kept printing. In this one, he wore glasses. "Steve, you really should watch for him. We all know what he looks like. We've seen this picture hundreds of times. I'll bet that there are more people in Boston who'd recognize that picture than a picture of the mayor or the governor."

"Holly, it's that same old black-and-white photo from six or eight years ago. They use the same three pictures all the time. This one. The one without glasses. And then there's that same shot with a moustache drawn on it."

"That one really is stupid. It looks as if a kid had scribbled on it."

"Probably doesn't matter," Steve said, "because there's nothing distinctive about him. Average guy. Medium height. Medium build. How old is he now? Late sixties? Gray hair."

"Blue eyes."

"Right. The next time I walk into the waiting room and see a gray-haired man with blue eyes, I'll call the FBI."

But he was amused. As I was feeling happy about flirting with him, however, a new segment of the Blackie special appeared on the screen. It opened with footage of my client and kidnapper, Enzio Guarini, as he walked toward the front door of his vegetation-free house in Munford. When he reached the door, he turned to the camera, smiled, and waved. He had good reason to look pleased. According to the voice-over, he was arriving home following his release from prison, his convictions having been thrown out at the prosecutors' request. Specifically, investigators from the Justice Department had come upon evidence in the Boston office of the FBI to suggest that Guarini had been framed by corrupt Boston agents acting in conjunction with former FBI informant James "Blackie" Lanigan. Guarini's conviction had rested heavily on the testimony of one of Blackie's underlings, a hit man named John O'Brian, whose body had subsequently been unearthed from the banks of the Neponset River. The testimony of another of Blackie's associates, a man now

in the Witness Protection Program, implicated Blackie
Lanigan as O'Brian's killer.

"Old news," Steve said. "Blackie got O'Brian to frame
Guarini, and then Blackie killed O'Brian to make sure
O'Brian couldn't turn around and testify about it."

"Corruption in the Boston FBI office isn't exactly news,
either," I said. "Everyone knows that Blackie was a so-
called informant for years, meaning that he kept doing
everything he'd always done, only he never got prose-
cuted, and he had the wonderful opportunity to inform
on his competition."

But the "Where's Blackie" program finally explained
its recap of old news by suggesting that the answer to
the ubiquitous question of Blackie Lanigan's whereabouts
was right here in Boston. The show switched to an interview with a reporter for one of the Boston papers, a
guy who specialized in the Mob and had written a book
about organized crime and its ties to Boston FBI agents.
According to the reporter, Enzio Guarini was bitter about
his incarceration, which he correctly blamed on Blackie
Lanigan. By alluding to La Cosa Nostra's reputation for
vendettas, the reporter managed to avoid claiming outright that the first thought on Guarini's mind when he'd
been released from prison had been to revenge himself on
Blackie. As to Blackie Lanigan's probable response to
Guarini's liberation, the reporter put a question to the
viewers: "Who'd you rather have after you? The FBI? Or
Enzio Guarini?" He gave his own answer. "Me, I'd take
the FBI any day."

Me, too, I thought.

"So Blackie's in Boston to get in a preemptive strike," Steve said. "If Guarini doesn't kill him first."

"Makes sense," I said, without adding that what now made perfect sense to me was Enzio Guarini's evident paranoia. No wonder Guarini traveled with those bodyguards. And Joey's killing? No wonder Guarini had seen it as a message to himself. When he'd ordered his men to get him the name of the shooter, he'd probably been asking them to find out who was working for Blackie Lanigan.

My eyes darted to Zap, who was still at the bar. He was hunched over a plate of fried food and sipping a beer. His face was without expression. You couldn't even tell whether he liked or disliked the food and drink. Zap's emotional deadness, though, was no concern of mine. I worried about Zap not for his sake but for the sake of my fragile relationship with Steve. If Zap turned and saw me, he wouldn't be stupid enough to stroll over to our table to chitchat about the bullet hole in Joey Cortiniglia's head. But he might be stupid enough to mention Enzio Guarini, his boss. *The* boss. *Our* boss.

"So," I said to Steve, "what do you feel like doing now, handsome? Any plans for the rest of the evening? How about popping into the nearest baggage claim and picking up a dog?"

CHAPTER 6

"The Love Song of J. Alfred Prufrock." You know the poem? T. S. Eliot. Well, if you haven't read it, take my advice and don't, because it's just line after horribly depressing line about the bleak existence of a man who is probably best remembered for having measured out his life with coffee spoons. And there you have what was wrong with J. Alfred Prufrock. I, in contrast, was blessed to have measured out my life with dogs. So was Steve Delaney.

All this is by way of saying that in Steve Delaney's life, as in mine, the arrival of the puppy was not the mere acquisition of a pet, but an Advent, a spiritual milestone, a reference point that would henceforth divide the calendar of his years into Before and After. Consequently, although the signs directing us to the baggage claim bore no resemblance to stars, I nonetheless felt like one of the Three Wise Men and, in fact, bore a gift. There were differences, certainly. For one thing, I'm a woman, and for another, *wise* was a bit of an exaggeration. If asked, I'd've settled for *knowledgeable*. My gift was a small hunk of roast beef. When it comes to dogs, I really am knowledgeable. Case in point: In a life spent in the company of canines, I had yet to meet a puppy who gave a sweet dog damn about gold, myrrh, or frankincense. Come to think of it, had the infant Jesus been all that crazy about such wildly inappropriate baby presents? Jesus, I'm sure, had been more than capable of remembering that it's the thought that counts. Steve's puppy would take beef over intentions any day.

When I say that Steve and I waited at the baggage claim, I don't mean that we watched for a puppy-size airline crate to drop down onto a conveyor belt among suitcases twice its size. Rather, we waited nearby until a rolling metal door surged upward to reveal a small shipping crate plastered with Live Animal stickers, This Way Up arrows, a small transparent envelope of airline paperwork, and, sealed under clear tape, a sheet of paper with information about who was sending the puppy to whom and instructions about what to do if the puppy got marooned somewhere.

Although auras are invisible to me, I nonetheless saw a glow of happiness radiate all around Steve as he took slow, deliberate steps forward, hunkered down, peered thoughtfully through the wire mesh door of the crate, and finally unlatched the little door. After the long hours alone in a crate in the cacophonous belly of an airliner, any small animal could have been excused for shyness, anxiety, or even outright post-traumatic stress. Not this little guy! When Steve eased the wire door open a scant two inches, a black nose thrust its eager way out, and immediately, catching Steve entirely off guard, the rest of the baby malamute followed. With the confidence built over years of handling wiggly little creatures, Steve enveloped Rowdy's young son in a bear hug and then sank his face into the soft coat on top of the puppy's head. Caught between an overwhelming urge to get my hands on the puppy and an absolute unwillingness to intrude on the bonding, I compromised by reaching out a hand and resting it on the pup's back. Under his soft puppy coat were hard bone and muscle that foretold the power he'd pack as an adult. His ribs rose and fell under my hand. Then, as if responding in kind to Steve's ursine hug, he scrambled up Steve's chest like a little bear climbing a big tree. When his face reached Steve's, he nibbled and licked, and his miniature tail whipped back and forth. He had Rowdy's blocky muzzle and Rowdy's perfect pigment and Rowdy's bittersweet-chocolate eyes. When Steve carefully lowered him to the floor, I could see that this miniature Rowdy was going to have his father's excellent bone as well.

Admiringly, Steve said, "Even better than your pictures, aren't you, big boy?"

"It's amazing," I said. "He already looks exactly like—"

For once, Steve interrupted. "Cindy didn't tell you? She told me. Little male version of Emma. Perfect pigment, blocky muzzle, heavy bone. Just like his mother."

"May I point out that Rowdy has perfect pigment? Not to mention a blocky muzzle, heavy bone . . . but, of course, Emma does go back to the same lines Rowdy does, on her mother's side. That's one reason Cindy wanted to use him."

With a shy smile, Steve said, "The universal affliction."

"Are you suggesting that I of all people am *kennel blind?* Objectively speaking, this puppy is a carbon copy of Rowdy."

Sensibly changing the subject, the duplicate little Rowdy began to sniff and circle in the universal manner of puppies who may not yet realize that they need to go out, but who certainly do.

"Hurry! I'll get the crate. I'll meet you just outside the door." I pointed to a nearby exit.

With Rowdy's son safely in his arms, Steve sprinted off. It took me only a moment to shut the door of the crate, which was pint-size by comparison with the ones I used for Rowdy and Kimi, so small that it had a handle on top. Carrying the crate by the handle, I made my way to the exit Steve had taken, but as I was about to go through the door, Zap appeared. This time, he noticed me.

"Hey," he said, "you get the message?"

Having seen all three Godfather movies, I broke into a sweat. I knew everything about Sicilian messages and was acutely aware that they weren't ordinary, innocent reminders like *Remember to pick up milk* or *Call me when you get a chance.* "What message was that?"

"About Joey's funeral. The boss wants you there 'cuz it's soon and a lot of people might not show up. I'm here picking up his sister, but her plane's late."

"Mr. Guarini's sister?"

"Joey's sister. For the funeral."

"This is the first I've heard about it."

"You didn't get the message."

"No. I haven't been home. I've been here." Duh.

"The boss is sending a car for you. Wear black."

"Enzio Guarini, fashion consultant," I blurted out.

Zap cracked a smile.

"When?" I asked.

"Ten o'clock."

"What *day*?"

"Tomorrow."

"And wear black." In what I intended as a be-seeing-you tone, I added, "Thanks."

For once, Zap remembered his manners or possibly forgot his lack thereof. Instead of departing, he held the exit door open for me. Short of telling him to leave, there was no way to get rid of him.

The door led to one of those nightmarish airport visions of a cement and asphalt future. Between the ugly concrete building I'd just left and the identical one opposite ran a blacktop road packed with buses, vans, cars, and diesel fumes. Overhead, rust-stained concrete walkways linked the terminals. *Terminal.* The mot juste, I always think. The world seems doomed to end neither with a bang nor a whimper but with a deadly boring wait in a concrete and asphalt airport that covers the entire surface of the planet, thus making it unnecessary to fly from anywhere to anywhere because you're already in the same gruesome place you'd go. But there was one sign of hope. Remember the one God sent to Noah? Not the rainbow. The other one. I'm convinced that *dove* is a mistranslation. But the first two letters are right.

In the wasteland of the airport Ararat, there had appeared the same sign God sent to Noah, and the people saw it, and they saw that it was good, which is to say the puppy, now wearing a little red collar attached to a red cotton leash, had drawn a clucking and ooh-ing crowd into which I hoped Zap would sink. He did not. Far from it. Rising to the top, Guarini's driver said, "Hey, you, what the hell are you doing with the boss's dog?"

I simply had to intervene. "This isn't Frey. This is a malamute puppy. See the white feet? And legs? The white on the face? Elkhounds are all gray. You see this puppy's tail? It's not curled. This is not an elkhound. This is not Frey." Without pausing, I added, "Steve, this is Zap. Zap, Steve. I'm, uh, training an elkhound puppy that belongs to a, uh, friend of Zap's, and—"

Zap cut me off by addressing Steve. "He's gonna be big. Look at the paws. That's how you tell. By the paws."

This to Steve Delaney, D.V.M., who nodded politely.

"How much you pay?" Zap demanded.

I answered. "A fair price, but the puppy is not—"

Zap asked the inevitable, "How much you want for him?"

In a tone that brooked no dispute, Steve said, "This is my dog. He's not for sale." With that, he swooped up

Rowdy's son. Nodding at Zap, he said, "Nice to meet you," and took off.

In parting, Zap said loudly, "Tomorrow at ten. Don't forget."

When I caught up with Steve, he repeated, "Tomorrow at ten?"

I said, "I have a very classy clientele these days. Maybe you noticed."

"No one could miss it."

"Tomorrow at ten," I said, "I'm training his friend's dog."

Incredible though it may seem, that was, in fact, what I ended up doing. The dog wasn't Frey. Still, at Joey Cortiniglia's funeral, I really did end up training a dog.

CHAPTER 7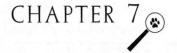

The interment of Joseph Ignatio Cortiniglia took place at a Roman Catholic cemetery in Munford. Joey's graveside service was the first I'd attended in ages. My father's intense response to my mother's death, in combination with my own grief, had left me petrified of funerals. In the past few years, I'd gone to a couple of blessedly bodiless memorial services, and strictly from a distance, I'd observed burials at the famous Mount Auburn Cemetery in Cambridge. But I'd successfully avoided actually attending all manner of decedent-present ceremonies. I was as frightened as ever. I went anyway. The only thing I had to fear was not fear itself. It was Enzio Guarini.

Joey's shiny wooden coffin was the centerpiece of the event. Suspended just above the grave, ready to be lowered into the earth, it was surrounded on all sides by fake-grass carpeting on which stood a small number of people and at least two dozen large and elaborate flower arrangements, indescribably immense floral wreaths displayed on easel-like stands, and ostentatious sheaves of oversize lilies and gladioli in extra large papier-mâché vases. The coffin was bedecked with rosebuds, baby's breath, and other selections that struck me as oddly delicate tributes to the brutish Joey Cortiniglia, whose living presence would've been more vividly evoked by big orange poppies with coarse, weedy foliage than it was by all this pink and white fragility.

Still, the lavishness of the flowers compensated for the sparse human attendance by creating the illusion that Joey Cortiniglia was mourned by a great many people, even though most of them weren't there. Enzio Guarini, of course, was there, together with his entourage: the two silent bodyguards, Alphonse "The Count" Favuzza, Zap the Driver, and the twin body movers, as I thought of them, the identical monstrosities who'd helped lift Joey's body into the Suburban and who'd mopped his blood and brains from the blacktop. Guarini's men all wore dark suits, but Al Favuzza, with his widow's peak, vampirish build, and Transylvanian aura, looked as if he'd just arisen from the flower-strewn coffin and might fall down dead at any moment from the lethal effects of the bright April sunshine. The wizened priest was so ancient that I wouldn't have been surprised to see him die of old age then and there. He kept glancing at Guarini as if seeking permission to begin the service. Two pallbearers hovered, and a round-bellied bald man kept going up to Guarini to ask, I felt certain, whether everything was all right. There were a handful of other men I'd never seen before, including two who stood a few yards away from everyone else. So far, they'd spoken to no one, and no one had spoken to them.

Anyway, it was the women who did most of the talking. Joey's sister, whose late-arriving plane had kept Zap at the airport, was sadly easy to identify, because she shared Joey's Ice Age features: the prognathous jaw, the brow ridge. As if to draw attention to her atavistic countenance, she'd slicked her long dark hair away from her face and fastened it with a big butterfly-shaped barrette. Either she hadn't received a message from Guarini, or hers had been different from mine. She wore aquamarine. I wore black. My dress was an old wide-wale corduroy shirtwaist I'd dug out of the back of the closet. Joey Cortiniglia's widow wore black, too. The sateen was as heavy as my out-of-season corduroy, but there ended the resemblance. Hers was a cocktail dress with thin straps and a plunging neckline that would've been revealing but for the presence of a tiny, fluffy dog tucked into her décolletage. Try that with a malamute. The minuscule creature belonged to no identifiable breed, but appeared to be a mix of Chinese crested and Yorkshire terrier with a dash of toy poodle and the merest soupçon of Chihuahua. The animal's most notable characteristics, however, were its ability to emit an amplified version of the sound of fingernails on a blackboard and its determination to exercise that ability nonstop. Because the tiny little squealer al-

most disappeared between the expanse of Mrs. Cortiniglia's very large, sateen-sheathed breasts, it would have
been easy to overlook the true source of the noise and to
imagine that Joey's widow was uniquely equipped with
a highly vocal bosom. With her mouth, she didn't need
one.

"Joey, Joey, I should've never let you eat all that crap!
Ham, pork roast, pork chops, and in your coffee, you
hadda have cream, not even half-and-half."

Joining her sister-in-law in this cholesterol-laden eu-
logy, Joey's sister managed to make herself heard above
the screaming of the little dog. "And butter. You ever
see Joey eat a piece of toast? Butter! All butter. And take
breakfast. Bacon and eggs, and I says to him, 'Look, Joey,
you're Italian, for Christ's sake, you never heard of the
Mediterranean diet? Olive oil, Joey, screw all this butter,
but—"

"On toast?" the widow asked.

"Carla, you always gotta take everything literally?"

"Jeannine, shut up!" Lowering her chin, Carla gave the
same order, long overdue, to the shrieking dog. "And you
shut up, too, Anthony!"

Al Favuzza, standing on my left, murmured something.
The only word I caught was *disrespect.*

After summoning the obsequious funeral director with
one pointed glance, Guarini apparently gave the go-ahead
for the service to begin. The funeral director whispered
in the priest's ear. Fumbling with a small black book, the
priest found his page and began to move his lips, but I
couldn't hear him over the renewed yapping and scream-

ing of Carla's little dog, Anthony. The other people all seemed to follow the service, despite Anthony's mockery of choir music; people crossed themselves in unison and showed no difficulty in responding whenever the inaudible priest paused. I kept my head respectfully bowed, while simultaneously watching Guarini in case he wanted me to do something about the dog. Indeed, it occurred to me that the obnoxious dog might be the real reason Guarini had wanted me here, possibly because I was one of the few people on earth capable of calmly removing the dog from Joey's last rites instead of strangling the damned thing.

Guarini didn't so much as look at me. The dog kept barking. Just in back of me, two women I didn't know conducted an off-again, on-again criticism of the proceedings.

"No viewing! No wake! What kind of crummy idea of a funeral is that?"

"Mavis, shut up," her companion said. "It's a beautiful day for a funeral, and the flowers are beautiful. Carla loves flowers, you know."

"Well, if Carla hadn't been in such a hurry to get him in the ground," Mavis said, "there'd be a decent crowd of people here to look at them."

"Would you not say *ground*?" the first woman said. "Who wants to think about it?"

Al Favuzza grunted in apparent agreement. Turning my head, I saw that the Count's face was green. Beads of sweat dotted his forehead.

Feeling like the funeral director, I asked, "Are you all right?"

Mavis, meanwhile, was saying, "Fact are facts! I mean, your soul goes to heaven or wherever, but your body—"

Without saying a word, Favuzza sidled away from me, ran a short distance, and took refuge behind a tombstone. At that precise moment, Carla's tiny dog, Anthony, finally fell silent, his screams replaced by the sounds of Favuzza's retching. The priest seemed to be reaching the end of the brief service. The undertaker had moved toward the coffin. The widow, Carla, had removed the dog from her bosom and was now clutching him in her hands. Suddenly, with a wail, she took up the lament she'd begun earlier. "Joey, Joey, Joey, what am I gonna do? How am I gonna live without you?"

Behind me, Mavis or her companion whispered, "Drama queen. She rents too many videos."

"Joey, I should've never let you eat like that," Carla went on. "I should've taken better care of you. What am I gonna do now?"

One of the funeral reviewers behind me murmured an answer. "Run a flower shop. Enzio's buying Carla a flower shop, you know that? She's going to be a florist."

"Joey!" Carla persisted. "I can't live without you!" With that, still clinging to the little dog, Carla made as if to throw herself onto Joey's coffin and thus presumably into the ground with him. Before actually hurling herself forward, however, she flashed her eyes left and right. Only after having verified the presence of Guarini's troops did she launch herself coffinward. Guarini's bodyguards made no move to stop her. Who says it's hard to get good help these days? If you're a Mob boss, it can still be done. The bodyguards concentrated on Guarini and left it to the gargantuan twins to prevent Carla from committing suttee. With the same big, capable hands they'd so recently used to wrap Joey in plastic and raise his corpse, they grabbed Carla's bare arms, thus triggering a fit of screaming and sobbing. They probably didn't mean to hurt her. Still, Carla's cries suddenly conveyed genuine pain, and—involuntarily, I'm sure—she released her grip on Anthony.

Fanciers of toy breeds are convinced that these little guys are exceptionally attuned to their owners. More than Rowdy and Kimi are to me? I doubt it. Still, it's true that when the bruisers put the brakes on Carla's rush to Joey's coffin, her toy dog gave every appearance of acting on her wishes by rocketing through the air and landing in the blossoms in the center of Joey's coffin. The gravediggers had cleverly sized the opening in the ground to be just a bit longer and wider than its intended contents, and the pseudo-grass carpet masked the gap between the earth and the box. No matter how effectively disguised, the gap had to be there. And the dog was as small as a kitten.

Drama queen no more, Carla was in a panic. "No! No! Anthony! He'll be buried alive! He'll fall six feet under! No!"

Guarini caught my eye and pointed a finger at me.

You see? Good help isn't hard to find. Without pausing to beg anyone's pardon, I pushed my way to Carla

and in a Don Corleone tone spoke to the men who re-
strained her. "Take her far away."

My black corduroy dress was one I'd never liked. I
couldn't remember the last time I'd worn it. The dog
treats in the pockets had held up well; the liver had been
freeze-dried to begin with. I crushed a couple of morsels
and rubbed my hands together to coat them with what I
hoped would be the irresistible scent of meat. As Guarini's men led Carla away, the little dog, Anthony, quit
his prancing to watch her departure. Calmly and quietly,
I managed to block his view of his retreating mistress.
Anthony stood on his four tiny paws in the exact center
of the coffin. If I'd tried to grab him, he'd probably have
evaded my grasp, run, and ended up falling underground.
Still, I had to suppress the impulse to snatch at him as
well as the urge to look him straight in the eye and try
to boss him around. Instead, I slowly reached out and
placed a bit of liver about a foot from the end of the
coffin. I kept my hand there, palm up, motionless, as if
I'd forgotten to remove it. Murmuring to myself in
happy, almost inaudible, tones, I fixed my gaze on the
liver. Old trainer's trick: To get a dog to move from one
place to another, instead of staring at the dog, stare at
the place you want him to go. Never having had the
opportunity to wise up to dog trainer wiles, Anthony
danced across the coffin and lowered his nose to the liver.
The hand I'd so carefully and so casually left there
wrapped itself firmly around Anthony's belly. "Gotcha,"
I said. "Good dog."

Thus ended both my capture of Anthony and the fu-

neral rites of Joseph Cortiniglia. I didn't wait to watch
as the Last of the Cave People—except one, his sister
Jeannine—was lowered into the earth. Joey's widow,
Carla, probably should've seen her husband out, but she
was busy getting her dog back. Carla was gratifyingly
profuse in her thanks. She said that whenever Anthony
got away from her, all he did was run away; never once
had she been able to catch him. "Have I, Anthony? You're
too fast for Mummy, aren't you? Aren't you? Anthony
doesn't like to come when Mummy calls . . ."

My stomach turned. I like dogs: great and small, including really small. The one who made me queasy was
Carla, who was holding Anthony out in front of her and
babbling at him as if he were a stuffed animal or a fig-
urine. The poor dog was lucky that Carla hadn't made
him wear a dress.

"We've been a naughty boy today, haven't we? We got
our lovely new velvet suit all wet and messy, so we
couldn't wear it."

In the hope of being rescued from Carla, I looked toward the tombstone behind which Al Favuzza had taken
shelter from the discussion of bodies and ground. But
Guarini appeared at my elbow. "Good," he said.

"I aim to please."

Carla cut me off by bursting into tears and wailing
self-evident truths about Joey: He was gone. He was really
gone. We'd never see him again. Then she switched to
bawling about her gratitude to Enzio. She didn't know
what she'd do without him. He was a good man. He was
a wonderful man. He was a man with a sense of family.

Then she did a tear-choked encore of her song about me. "This lady's a genius! If she hadn't've been there, Anthony . . . well, it would've been awful. Anthony won't listen to a word I say."

Guarini's response horrified me. "Holly can fix that," he assured Carla. He eyed me.

"Oh, yes," I said. "I'd be delighted."

CHAPTER 8

"Where've you been? A Mafia funeral?" Rita thought she was joking.

As my dear friend as well as my second-floor tenant, Rita knew all about my phobia. Come to think of it, as a clinical psychologist, Rita undoubtedly knew my whole inner life better than I did. She'd been walking down Appleton Street toward our shared driveway when Guarini's limo had dropped me off. For once, I'd been anything but happy to see her, mainly because psychotherapy was not just her profession, but her calling in life; she always felt spiritually compelled to ask personal questions and was constitutionally incapable of believing that something—anything—could be none of her damned business. When Zap had stopped the limo, Al Favuzza had stepped out and held the door for me. Even more than

Guarini himself or any of his other henchmen, Al Favuzza looked like a mobster. He looked more like a mobster than he did like a vampire, and that's saying something. Naked, right out of the shower, Favuzza probably looked as if he were carrying a concealed weapon. I wouldn't have put it past him to do just that. Ugh. Let's skip over the possibilities.

Adopting Rita's tone, I said, "It's a new hobby of mine. I've overcome my phobia. Now I flit from funeral to funeral without a twinge of the old panic. As you've no doubt observed, the transportation is nothing short of elegant, and I am becoming a connoisseur of floral tributes."

"I like your dress," Rita said. "It's so cheerful and springlike." Rita wore a yellow linen suit with good shoes. She is so un-Cambridge. I'm one Cambridge type: denim and T-shirts. Another is ethnic: Peruvian hats. Another is expensive jersey drapery with chunky handcrafted jewelry. Rita is pure New York: style before comfort.

I fingered the dowdy black corduroy. " 'April is the cruelest month,' you know."

"May I ask what you've been up to?"

"A pun! May. April. Rita, how unlike you!"

"You're avoiding something. Black dress, Cadillac limousine. *Bela Lugosi Meets the Godfather?*"

Rita's professional time may truly be worth what she charges for it. "Do not mention any of this to Kevin. And do *not* tell Steve, either. Don't tell anyone. You want some coffee? Lunch?"

One of Rita's patients had canceled, so she had time to accept my invitation. When I'd let the dogs out into the fenced yard, made coffee, seated Rita at my kitchen table, and spread it with sandwich fixings, I told her the entire story of my association with Enzio Guarini. I wasn't about to waste the free availability of Rita's expensive therapeutic ear by spilling anything less than the full, absolute truth. I omitted not one single thing . . . except the small matter of Joey Cortiniglia's manner of death. Guarini had told me that it hadn't happened. Therefore, it hadn't.

Rita isn't normally the kind of therapist—or friend—who limits herself to um-ing and nodding and asking how you feel about things. Consequently, I was surprised when she asked how I felt. To be specific, she said, "Enzio Guarini is a notorious criminal. He is a racketeer and a loan shark and a multiple murderer, for a start, and the only reason he's out of jail is corruption in the Boston office of the FBI. How do you feel about accepting money from a person like that?"

"Rita, I am helping him with his puppy. You make it sound as though I've switched from dog training to contract killing. What I am is Dog, Incorporated, not Murder, Incorporated." In case you, too, wondered, let me state that as a matter of pride, I hadn't taken Guarini's money. "Since when did you become so big on inducing guilt?"

"Holly, that's blood money. It's ill-gotten gains."

I chose not to tell Rita that I was a volunteer. "Rita, my car is falling to pieces. It is a hazard and an embarrassment. I have two big dogs to feed, not to mention myself."

"Such martyrdom! And when did you suddenly start

earning a living by training other people's dogs?"

"I've helped people with their dogs before."

"People who adopted dogs from Malamute Rescue. Do you charge those people?"

"No, but I've coached people who were starting to show in obedience."

"A handful of times."

"I am perfectly qualified."

"Of course you are. This isn't a matter of qualifications. It's a matter of ethics. Holly, why would you have anything to do with scum like Enzio Guarini?"

"I'm scared to death of him."

"Talk to Kevin."

"No! Look, Rita, I can handle this. I have a plan. I just go along with Guarini. I train his puppy, Frey. I help Guarini to work with Frey. Guarini actually knows a lot about dogs. It's just that the puppy has more energy than he does, and Guarini's approach is old-fashioned. When it comes to puppy training, he's out of date."

"I wonder why that is," Rita said snidely.

I ignored the remark. "And once the puppy is shaped up, that's that. I'm done. I never have to see Guarini again."

"And that's why you've just come from a funeral."

"You want me to stay phobic? Here before your psychotherapeutic eyes, the forces of mental health are triumphing over neurosis, and your only response is to be negative and critical?"

"I hope you know what you're doing."

"I do. And do *not* mention any of this to Steve."

"Speaking of—"

"Rita, I have to tell you, his puppy is so beautiful. He's called Sammy. He looks so much like Rowdy you can hardly believe it."

"I was starting to ask about *Steve*."

"Rita, Steve is a real dog person. If you ask *him* how he is, he'll tell you about his dogs."

"So if I want to hear how *he* is, I need to ask about his dogs? So, how are Steve's dogs?"

"Fine. The puppy is wonderful. Steve called early this morning to say that he'd introduced the puppy to India, and things went well. Lady wasn't an issue. She accepted Sammy right away."

"Does there exist a way for me to find out how *Steve* is?"

"His dogs are fine. There's your answer. If they're fine, he's fine. He's crazy about the puppy. Therefore, he's more than fine."

"Steve's dogs were fine last summer. And last fall. He wasn't."

"The core of his being *was*. He'd just been temporarily led astray by bad companions. Or one bad companion."

"Whom he married."

"I *said* he was led astray. He was led *far* astray."

"I don't want to force you to talk about things you're uncomfortable talking about. I just hope you're dealing with them in your own way. When is his divorce going to be final?"

"I don't know. And my own way of dealing with things is via dogs, and that's Steve's way, too."

Rita rolled her eyes.

"Look, Rita, I know I sound defensive."

She waved her hands in the air in a gesture of brushing my words aside. "Not at all."

"Spare me the sarcasm. Look, if I'd listened to you, none of it would've happened. You told me over and over that I was taking Steve for granted. You told me that the consistent message I gave him was that my dogs came first and that he got whatever time and energy were left over. You quoted the song: 'A Good Man Is Hard to Find!'"

"A good man *is* hard to find," Rita said.

"I know that. Now."

"And?"

"And how things are with Steve and me is fragile. Delicate. We are heartbreakingly considerate of each other. We are afraid of intruding. All the old comfort is gone, except that we still know each other so well. Also, weirdly enough, we have fun together. At least we did at Logan when we picked up Sammy. And I know you're going to say that anyone can have fun, but—"

"Not so! Fun is a good sign. Laughter is good for you."

"Didn't Nietzsche say something about laughter and the death of the soul?"

"Nietzsche," said Rita, "was crazy. That's my professional opinion. Besides, Nietzsche is dead."

So, of course, was Joey Cortiniglia, as reported in a short paragraph buried (sorry) in the middle of that day's newspaper, which I skimmed after Rita returned to the miserable task of sitting in her office listening to people whine. Here's what the paper said:

REPUTED MOB ASSOCIATE DIES

Joseph "Little Joey" Cortiniglia (36) died of a heart attack on Tuesday. Cortiniglia was rumored to have ties to recently released alleged organized crime boss Enzio Guarini. Cortiniglia had been convicted only once, for running a dice game. Guarini refused comment on Cortiniglia's death except to say that Cortiniglia was a respectable citizen and businessman. Cortiniglia headed a pest control company in Munford.

So there you have it: the official story of Joey's death from what I knew damn well to be a reported, reputed, rumored, alleged, thoroughly fictitious, fabricated, and imaginary heart attack. In a peculiar way, Guarini had once again gotten away with murder.

CHAPTER 9

That night, I dreamed that my beat-up old Bronco was parked in the middle of a vast stretch of otherwise empty blacktop. Rowdy and Kimi were hitched to its undercarriage. Just as in real life, they were gnawing on big beef bones. Prone on the asphalt, I raised what felt like a heavy hand to my head. My fingers encountered a big, wet bullet hole. Both dogs stopped chewing and stared at me, their eyes brimming with trust. I awoke with the realization that the head with the bullet hole could have been mine instead of Joey's. I absolutely had to rid myself of the Mob. The sooner I transformed Frey into the perfect canine companion, the sooner I'd be free of Guarini.

The boss had been right to be wary of public places. Furthermore, what had felt like his senseless prohibition on puppy kindergarten now seemed sensible. Somehow, I'd have to socialize and train Frey without becoming a Sicilian message to Enzio Guarini. As I finished my second cup of morning coffee, I jotted down an intensive training plan for Frey. Rowdy and Kimi, seeing my edginess, watched me with the same trust I'd felt from them in the dream. With regard to dog training, their trust was well placed. I told them so. "When it comes to people," I said, "I'm perfectly likely to bungle things, but I do know how to train dogs. No public places? We'll create them here. No puppy kindergarten? We'll do our own." I picked up the phone and called Steve at his clinic. "How you doing?" I asked.

Proving the point I'd made to Rita, he said, "Sammy is quite a character." Steve went on to report that India was mothering Sammy and that Lady was afraid of him. Steve and I agreed that since Lady was afraid of everything, her reaction was normal, at least for her.

"What've you been up to?" he asked with an attempt at casualness.

"Up to?" I replied, thinking of Guarini. "Nothing! Nothing at all! Not a thing. Not one thing." Coming to my senses, I said, "Actually, I'm training a puppy who needs socialization, and it occurred to me"—a gross understatement—"that I could do a sort of mini puppy class here with him and Sammy. Basic socialization. Puppy play. Fun stuff. Very carefully supervised. I don't believe in leaving puppies free to practice bad behavior. You interested?"

After making sure that Frey had been thoroughly vet

checked and was free of contagious diseases and up to
date on his shots, Steve eagerly accepted the invitation.
Next I called Guarini, who again told me what good
work I'd done with Carla's coffin-dancing little fiend, Anthony.

"Elementary," I said modestly. "I have a new plan for
Frey. The story is that a friend of mine has a malamute
puppy, younger than Frey, and I want to get the puppies
together here. It's a great opportunity to socialize Frey."
Guarini agreed. The plan was that on prescheduled week-
day mornings, Steve or one of his assistants would drop
Sammy off here. At ten, Frey would arrive. He'd stay for
two hours of puppy play and training before being limoed
home. I'd then return Sammy to Steve's, or keep him with
me. Steve would never run into Guarini's men. In the
two hours Frey was with me, I could do multiple brief
training sessions with him. And, of course, I'd get to
spend time with Rowdy's little son. Perfect! For the rest
of the day, I puppy-proofed the house, set up crates, and
assembled supplies. While I was at it, I put together a
puppy-training lesson plan for Guarini to use with Frey.

Holly's Puppy School opened its door the next morning
when Sammy the malamute barged into my kitchen right
on schedule. Rowdy and Kimi were in their crates in my
bedroom. Why? Because when it comes to malamutes,
true love means deep understanding, which means profound mistrust; I intended to introduce Rowdy and Kimi
to Sammy one grown-up dog at a time, very gradually
and very carefully. First, the big dogs would get used to

the scent of Sammy in their house, as they were doing
this morning.

Sammy busied himself distributing that scent. His
baby tail waving in the air, Sammy bounded and bounced
from room to room, corner to corner, lingering to sniff
and paw, then eagerly returning to the adventure of
puppy-mapping this brand new territory. Every puppy is
Neil Armstrong, and the planet Earth is every puppy's
moon.

Sammy's partner in exploration, Frey, arrived on schedule at ten, delivered by Zap, who failed to recognize
Sammy as the puppy he'd seen at Logan and asked how
much I wanted for him. When I'd sent Zap on his way,
my little pupils got a ten-minute recess in the fenced
yard, during which time I sat on the steps and watched
the boys play. At first, Frey hid under a bush, but Sammy
lured him out and before long, the two were the picture
of busyness as they engaged in hide and go seek without
the hide, in other words, tearing around for the joy of
tearing around. Except to work on housebreaking by offering praise and treats for going outside ("Good puppy!"),
I didn't have to step in at all. The mistake Guarini had
made in trying to housebreak Frey had been the common
one of letting him out. To house-train a puppy, you don't
just *let* him out. You *take* him out so you're right there
to reinforce the desired behavior.

After recess, Sammy had nap time in a pint-size crate,
while I worked with Frey on the fundamentals of canine
civilization: come, sit, down, stay. Guarini's pup and I
practiced off leash in my kitchen, in my living room, and

in my fenced yard; and on leash in my driveway. As I told Frey, he was brilliant, excellent, wonderful; he was my good dog, my good puppy, my good Frey. He learned quickly, and, in so doing, he was rapidly going to break my ties to his master. The puppies then got another run in the yard. When I'd crated the little ones, Rowdy and Kimi got to go outside. After returning the big dogs to their crates, I again worked with Frey, and then he and Sammy tore around. Finally, I leashed Frey, took him into the yard, and in calm, rewarding circumstances, introduced him to startling stimuli: a bicycle and a bicycle horn. Back in the house, Frey met Tracker, my cat.

Two hours of puppy home-schooling felt like twenty minutes. After Zap had picked up Frey, far from being tired, I was so energized that I whipped off a column for *Dog's Life* about the happy privilege of seeing the world through puppy eyes. In the late afternoon, Guarini and I did phone-assisted dog training. I sat at my kitchen table sipping coffee, scratching Rowdy under the chin, and talking to Guarini. The same capo who juggled racketeering, extortion, money laundering, and so forth somehow couldn't manage Frey, the clicker, the treats, and his cell phone all at once, so he used a speaker phone to listen to me coach him in attention training and in the basic obedience exercises Frey and I had practiced that morning. An advantage of helping an experienced dog person like Guarini was that he understood the importance of keeping the training session short and fun. He had a good voice for dogs, and his praise was genuine. I hoped that the successful day would set a pattern for the next few weeks, by the end of which Guarini would no longer need my help with Frey.

Feeling optimistic, I checked my E-mail. In addition to the usual zillion messages I always get from Malamute-L, Dogwriters-L, Caninebackpackers, a couple of obedience lists, and the list for members of the Alaskan Malamute Club of America, I had two personal messages. One message was from my friend Mary Wood, who lived in California. Mary's position in the malamute community—Family Redefined—was similar to mine. Mary had only two dogs, both malamutes, a male and a female. Like Rowdy and Kimi, Mr. Wookie and Miss Pooh were beloved house pets as well as show dogs. Mr. Wookie had rocketed to "mal-fame" at the age of fourteen months by winning Grand Sweepstakes the Alaskan Malamute National Speciality in Louisville, Kentucky. Rocketed? It was his *first* show. That's impressive. Now, like Rowdy, he was what's called a "specials dog"—a dog who has finished his championship and is competing for Best of Breed and stardom in the Working Group. Lots of people who campaign specials use professional handlers, but Mary Wood handled Mr. Wookie herself. Malamute people used to say that if Mary really wanted the dog to go places, she'd have to hire a professional. Mary silenced her critics by owner-handling Mr. Wookie to Best of Breed at the National Specialty and, soon thereafter, at the AKC/Eukanuba Classic. Showing Mr. Wookie was the point of Mary's E-mail. The two of them were coming to New England.

Mary gave me their jam-packed itinerary; no one trav-

els all the way from California to enter one show. Their
first show in this area was the Saturday after next. As I
told Mary in my E-mail reply, Rowdy and Kimi were
both entered. As I didn't tell her, with Mr. Wookie in
the ring, Rowdy was going to lose. Rowdy is a good dog
and a good show dog, but reality is reality, and the judge,
Harry Howland, had had Mr. Wookie in his ring before
and loved him every time. So why not leave Rowdy at
home? Because the more dogs Mr. Wookie defeated, the
higher he'd rise in the rankings, that's why. Yes, I'm a
good sport.

The second message was from Steve, who invited me
to dinner at Aspasia, a divine restaurant on Walden Street
only a block from my house. I E-mailed my acceptance.
A year earlier, when my relationship with Steve was in
its previous incarnation, it wouldn't have been a big deal
to go out to dinner with him. Let me rephrase that. Once,
long ago, back when I took Steve for granted, I'd have
made no big deal of going out with him. As a dog trainer,
I knew damned well that behavior was governed by its
consequences. The behavior in question: my taking Steve
for granted. The consequence: Steve's marrying someone
else, and not just anyone else, but Anita Fairley, an embezzler and a bitch, not that Steve knew about her criminal activities when he married her. As to her bitchiness?

Having resolved to modify my behavior, I subjected
myself to as thorough a grooming as the dogs get before
a show. Dog-minded as I was and am, I respected the
species differences. For example, I did not chalk my legs
with cornstarch and brush it out, but I did shave my legs

and even went so far as to neaten my nails, with an emery board, let me emphasize, not with Rowdy and Kimi's orange handled clippers. I did the whole bit: applied makeup, blew my hair dry. Cambridge being Cambridge, I could've worn anything from old jeans and a T-shirt to a floor-length velvet dress. Cambridge is big on options. Leaving options open is the basis of the arguments that Cambridge parents use in convincing their kids to attend the local college: Once you have your Harvard degree, dear, your options will be open. What the kids don't know is that Harvard crimson won't wash out; like shirts sent to a laundry that uses indelible ink, Harvard students stay marked for life.

But I'm avoiding the issue. Steve's soon-to-be ex-wife, Anita, was incredibly beautiful and wore expensive, fashionable clothes. Feeling like a jealous teenager, I pawed through the contents of my closet. Rowdy reduced my options by snatching a black skirt and running off with it. So long as he and Kimi didn't use it to play tug-of-war, it would survive, but it was already too thick with dog hair to wear. I settled on a gray skirt and top that were probably covered with malamute coat, but at least didn't show it. To the best of my recollection, I'd never seen Anita in gray. Have I mentioned that she hated dogs?

Where was I?

The new awkwardness between Steve and me had its limits; he didn't go so far as to make a formal appearance at the front door. When he entered the kitchen, Rowdy and Kimi did the malamute equivalent of falling all over him by wagging their entire bodies and emitting melodious, half-howled greetings, all the while fixing predatory eyes on the bouquet of delphiniums he held high above their reach.

"You've done something to your hair," he said. "You look nice."

"Thank you." In case the delphiniums were inexplicably for Rita instead of me, I didn't thank him for them. Also, I didn't return his compliment by telling him the truth about his own appearance, which was that he looked like a combination of Mel Gibson and the young Paul Newman.

"Aren't delphiniums the ones you like?"

"They're my favorites. They're beautiful. Thank you."

Delphiniums are toxic to dogs. So are many other ornamental plants, including, irony of ironies, holly. Luckily, Rowdy and Kimi had never shown any interest in vases of flowers.

"Thanks for having Sammy here."

"My pleasure. I'm crazy about Sammy. You can leave him here whenever you want."

Steve smiled. "Now? He's in my van."

"The puppy crate's right here. Rowdy and Kimi can stay in the . . ."

Bedroom.

I'm going to sound like Rita, but I have to say that our precautions about maintaining distance between Sammy and the adult dogs mirrored our concern about maintaining distance from each other. The chances were good that if turned loose with little Sammy, neither Rowdy nor Kimi would've hurt the puppy. And just how safe together were Steve and I?

CHAPTER 10

The dinner, and the expensive pinot noir we drank with it, induced in me an unfamiliar sense of contentment and optimism, especially about Steve. It is often said of companionable but discontented couples that the chemistry just isn't there. With us, the chemistry always had been there and still was. Furthermore, we'd never been and obviously wouldn't become one of those couples who disagreed about pets or fought about dogs. Dogs were, however, one of the reasons we'd never lived together. India, Steve's shepherd—German shepherd dog—wouldn't sacrifice her dignity by starting a dog fight, even with Kimi, whom India viewed as a threat to civilization as India knew it and liked it. Kimi, in turn, saw India as a complacent reactionary who'd been co-opted by the forces of repression and thus constituted a threat to the ultimate triumph of radical canine feminism. As to Kimi's views about Lady, Steve's pointer, Kimi showed a regrettable lack of sisterly feeling. Far from sympathizing with Lady's fearfulness, Kimi went out of her way to intimidate Lady by grabbing Lady's toys, barging ahead of her, and slamming into her as if by accident. India, who was nobly protective of Lady, would glare at Kimi, who'd return the silent warning with a snarl. Rowdy respected India and liked Lady, who was frightened of him and stayed out of his way. And Sammy? Two male malamutes might learn to coexist. Or might not. The Kimi-Sammy combo? But why on earth was I working out the possibilities of living with all five dogs when Steve and I, far from being on the verge of combining households, had merely advanced to sharing a table at a restaurant?

"How is that?" I referred to his main course, a trendy version of beef Wellington.

"Excellent. Outstanding." Steve was using his knife and fork with surgical precision. At the dinner table, as at the operating table, he was deft and neat. Around the house, too, Steve had always washed his own dishes. He'd never left piles of damp towels on the floor. He'd prepared and sorted the recyclables correctly. Not that the habit of depositing unrinsed bottles in the wrong bin would've made him hopelessly unforgivable; I probably have it in me to care deeply for someone who can't or won't follow simple directions. The point about Steve was that he was astoundingly considerate and didn't expect other people to clean up after him. The mess he'd made by marrying

Anita? He'd take full responsibility for tidying it up all by himself.

"How's yours?" he asked.

Asparagus risotto. The restaurant, Aspasia, was stylishly New American Mediterranean rather than Italian. In fact it was more Greek than it was Italian. Well, the menu really wasn't Italian at all. Not in the least. Except for the risotto. The item I'd chosen.

"Out of this world." I thought about offering him a taste from my fork, but settled for transferring a portion to his plate.

We talked about how lucky we were to have such a wonderful restaurant only a block from my house. Good food was Steve's only extravagance. He still lived in the apartment over his vet clinic and still drove the dog-scented van he'd had for years. Unlike my new acquaintances, he didn't wear flashy rings, gold chains, or ID bracelets. He'd never worn a wedding ring. The only thing remotely like jewelry he ever wore was a watch, and he wore it strictly to tell time, not to make a statement. Steve's idea of making a statement was saying outright exactly what he meant. Even my horrible cat loved him.

I thought about telling him that Tracker missed him, but was afraid that he'd correctly understand that the statement was more about me than about the cat. I also rejected the possibility of asking how his mother was. She wasn't giving to hissing and scratching in Tracker fashion. Still, the topic of difficult females could all too easily lead to the vile Anita, and I wanted to avoid referring to her at all. Naturally, I had questions about her ("So, is she going to end up in jail?") and about the end of their marriage ("How's the divorce progressing?"), but I suppressed them. The category of difficult females probably included me, too. At the moment, my ridiculous case of first-date nerves couldn't have been easy to take.

"The risotto is so creamy," I said. "It's delicious. I love the way it feels. . . ." I stopped there, without adding, "on my tongue."

Happily for my tongue-tied state, Rita and the man in her life, Artie Spicer, entered the restaurant just then. After greeting us, they were shown to a table far enough away from us to allow me to talk about them without being overheard, not that I had anything terrible to report or opine. Still, it would've been tactless to let Rita and Artie listen in as I dissected their romance in more or less the same way Steve was dissecting the beef Wellington. Rita was a friend of Steve's, and he knew Artie, too, so they involuntarily provided us with a topic of common interest, as I felt sure they'd have done voluntarily if they'd been asked. But you can hardly walk up to a couple and say, "We're having an awkward time and need a subject of conversation, and I was wondering whether you'd mind if we talked about you."

I, of course, was determined to discuss everything about Rita, Artie, and their relationship except the crucial matter of where it was heading, but Steve, as usual, eventually got to the point by asking, "Where do you think things are going with them?"

"I don't know."

"What does Rita say?"

"She says she doesn't know." After she'd said that, she'd go on to ask me where I thought things were going with Steve and me, and she'd press me about where I wanted things to go, but since I was having trouble talking easily with Steve about such emotionally neutral topics as risotto, I didn't feel ready to wonder aloud what we wanted from each other and whether it was even a good idea for us to be sitting here together ordering crème brûlée. When the dessert arrived, it felt luxuriously sensuous on my tongue. I interpreted the sensation as a good omen, but kept the prognostication to myself.

When we left the restaurant, light rain was falling. Steve took my hand, and with arms swinging, we almost danced along Concord Avenue, around the corner to Appleton Street, and up my driveway.

"You feel like a walk?" he asked.

"Yes. Sammy and Kimi?"

Kimi, not Rowdy, got to go on the walk with Sammy because of the weather. To an extraordinary degree, Rowdy possessed an Arctic dog's primitive and powerful defense against dying of hypothermia: He absolutely hated getting wet. Kimi didn't loathe rain with Rowdy's passionate intensity. According to Steve, little Sammy had not inherited his father's determination never to set paw outdoors on damp ground. While I changed into jeans, a sweatshirt, and rain gear, Steve got Sammy from his crate and set off for the corner of Concord Avenue and Walden Street, where we'd arranged to meet. Contrary to popular myth, adult dogs do not necessarily extend tolerance to puppies; on the contrary, in some cases, the adults maim or kill the puppies. Although Kimi already knew Sammy in the scent sense, since he'd been running all over the house, Steve and I had decided to abide by the policy of introducing Kimi and Sammy face-to-face on neutral territory, not in Kimi's own house or yard.

Kimi and I followed Steve and Sammy's route along Concord Avenue. Ignoring the traffic, Kimi did her bit for female liberation by repeatedly lifting her leg and kicking her heels in the air. From a half a block away, I saw Steve bending over Sammy, who was in that adorable stand-and-lean stance that male puppies use before hormones impel them to start imitating tough-minded female malamutes. As Kimi and I drew near, I could hear Steve murmuring the inevitable, "Good dog. Good puppy! Good boy." My eyes were on Kimi. Resisting the urge to tighten her leash, I concentrated on observing her response to Sammy. Misted by the rain, his fluffy puppy coat stood out as if he'd just been groomed. Catching sight of him, Kimi briefly halted. Her hackles stayed down, her ears perked up, and her face took on a wondrous expression of amazement, as if she were a disbeliever in magic who'd suddenly seen a unicorn. As if this angelic behavior were exactly what I'd expected, I said, "Good girl, Kimi. Sammy sure is cute, isn't he?"

The temptation, of course, was to let Kimi and Sammy run right up to each other.

"Give Kimi another minute or two," Steve said. "Let's walk. I'll keep Sammy just out of striking distance."

"Kimi's decided to like Sammy." Hearing me speak her name, she looked up at me, but rapidly transferred her attention back to Sammy, who was bouncing, pulling, running, halting, turning to look at the passing cars, and practically turning somersaults. Kimi regarded his antics with open curiosity.

"Okay, let's give it a try," Steve told me.

We decreased the distance between the dogs. Kimi trotted up to Sammy. She towered over him. Seeing just that, Sammy sensibly rolled onto his back on the sidewalk to present his underbelly. Like a dog pediatrician, Kimi gave him a brief but thorough exam. Then I stepped back, called her to me, and doled out a liver treat. "Perfect!" I was talking to Steve as well as to Kimi. Now that I think of it, I guess that in relating this meeting of the dogs, I'm talking about what was going on between Steve and me as well. Damn! This is what comes of hanging around with a psychotherapist. According to Rita, everything always has to be some kind of symbol or image or metaphor. Hah! I did not tower over Steve. He was not about to roll belly up.

We took our walk. With Sammy setting the pace, the so-called walk took us only a short distance down Walden Street. Reversing direction, the four of us returned to the corner of Walden and Concord and were heading home when we had a minor but unsettling encounter.

Because of the rain, hardly anyone else was out, and most of the people we'd seen had been hurrying. A few had paused briefly to smile at the puppy and say how cute he was. Heading toward us now was a woman shrouded in a dark rain poncho with the hood up. Accompanying her at the end of a long retractable leash was

a little dust mop of a dog, part shih tzu, part Lhasa, at a
guess, with maybe some cocker mixed in. Spotting the
new dog, Steve swooped Sammy up in his arms. As a vet,
Steve was an especially protective owner. Until Sammy
had had the last of his puppy shots, at about four months,
Steve wouldn't want him exposed to strange dogs. My
concern about Kimi had to do with aggression rather than
disease, but I immediately saw that there was no reason
to worry. Kimi was much better with other dogs than
she'd once been, and now, as the wet little dog scampered
toward her, she seemed relaxed, amiable, and altogether
happy to return what was clearly going to be a friendly
greeting. The cheery dust mop bounced and wiggled up
to Kimi, who returned the wiggle. If both dogs had been
waving white flags, the peaceful nature of their intentions
wouldn't have been more clear than they were now. At
the risk of repeating myself, I must stress that I, a human
being and therefore fallible, might've missed a warning
sign: a soft growl, an almost imperceptible raising of
hackles, or a subtle change in the little dog's respiration.
Kimi, however, would've noticed even the most elusive
cause for alarm.

There was none. One second, the little newcomer was
making friends. The very next second, this same harmless-
acting creature had darted underneath Kimi and was ripping into her underbelly. A sneak is one thing. But a dog
sneak! And a clever one. Fast, too.

In a dog crisis, I'm pretty quick myself. Before Kimi
could take revenge, I bent down over her and, with one
hand on her collar and the other under her chest, lifted

her up while addressing the poncho-clad owner. "Get your dog out of here now!"

The owner was about ten feet away. When she yanked off the hood of her poncho, I recognized the woman whose bicycle had scared Frey a few weeks earlier. She was a real Cambridge type. Perhaps sixty-five, she had a boney, intelligent face and short, straight gray hair cut in an unflattering Dutch boy clip. While retracting the leash, she apologized to me in Harvardian pseudo-British tones and scolded her dust mop in the same voice. "So dreadfully sorry! I can't imagine what got into her. Elizabeth Cady, bad girl! You had no reason whatsoever to display belligerence, did you? We'll toddle off back home this very minute and contemplate our sins. So terribly sorry." The retractable leash was now short, as it should've been all along. To my relief, the woman soon found a break in the traffic and led Kimi's pint-size attacker to the opposite side of Concord Avenue. Elizabeth Cady. Stanton. Pioneer advocate of women's rights. Cambridge, my Cambridge.

When we got back to my house, we ended the evening as soon as we'd made sure that Kimi was uninjured. Steve trained dogs, too. Both of us understood the importance of keeping sessions short and happy. If everything is going well, it's always tempting to push for yet more progress. That's a beginner's mistake. Steve and I weren't novices, especially with each other.

A few hours later, as I lay in bed awaiting sleep, I searched for a moral to what struck me as the parable or fable enacted that evening. Its title was evident: Kimi and the Dust Mop with Teeth. What eluded me was the moral. I wasn't alone in the king-size bed. Rowdy was asleep on the floor under the air conditioner, which on this cool April night was, of course, turned off. Savoring happy memories or dreaming of Arctic blasts, he was in a sled dog tuck, his body in a fetal curl, his tail wrapped over his nose. Kimi was stretched out on the bed, her spine pressed against mine. She was on top of the covers, not between the sheets. Steve wasn't between my sheets, either, but he was presumably between his own. I tried to take comfort in the thought that he and I were both between unspecified sheets and tried not to dwell on the separateness of our beds.

Kimi and the Dust Mop with Teeth.

What *was* the moral?

CHAPTER 11

It's hard being a mobster. You're always in danger of being shot, strangled, knifed, drowned, blown up, or imprisoned. Before my affiliation with the Mob, I'd heard about all those concrete perils. Household phrase: *Concrete boots.* What had escaped me was the weighty psycho-vocational burden of worrying about respect, disrespect, and the rest of that macho crap, all of which I already understood in depth: When it comes to machismo, a male human being can't hold even the most phallic candle to a male malamute and shouldn't try. Given the opportunity, Rowdy would probably wear flashy rings and get chauffeured around and rule over a pack of capos, advisors, and hit men. Come to think of it, as it is now, I supply Rowdy's expensive collars and leashes, I drive him around, I serve as his trusted advisor, and I act as his bodyguard.

A big chunk of my money goes to him. Never, ever would I betray him. Omerta: the code of silence about Rowdy's misdeeds. Holly Winter: capo, consigliere, and all the rest in one. Rowdy: *capo di tutti capi.*

What leads me to Mob angst and machismo, isn't, for once, my dogs, but a series of phone calls I received in the days following the dust mop's assault on Kimi's underbelly. I got the first of these calls the next morning. Rowdy and Kimi were in their crates, and the puppy boys, Frey the elkhound and Sammy the malamute, were studying a required subject in the puppy curriculum: aggression management via play. When the phone rang, Sammy was winning in tug-of-war with a long fleece snake. The thought crossed my mind that if I heard Guarini's voice, I probably shouldn't mention that Frey was losing to another pup. But the caller was a stranger, a man who said, with no preamble, "You the dog lady?"

I said yes.

"Mr. Guarini told me to call you. I got a problem with my dog."

In one of those abrupt shifts of interest to which puppies are given, Sammy and Frey had dropped the toy snake and were lapping noisily out of the same big water bowl.

Keeping an eye on the puppies, I grabbed a pen and paper. "Maybe I can help. Let's start with what kind of dog this is."

"He's a Doberman. But he don't act like one."

"How old is he?" I asked.

"A year."

"A male," I said. Ordinarily, my next question would've been, "And is he neutered?" Intuition told me to hold off. "And what's his name?"

"Durango."

"And what's up with Durango?"

"Like I said, he don't act like a Doberman."

"Could you, uh, be a little more specific? What is it that he *does*?"

"It ain't what he does. It's what he don't do. Except there's one thing, and I gotta tell you, this's driving me nuts. He lays down."

"And?"

"I put him in the car, and he just lays down."

"I'm sorry if I'm being dense, but I don't see what the problem is. A lot of dogs sleep in the car. If someone else is driving, I might sleep in the car. There's nothing wrong with that, is there?"

"But you ain't a Doberman!" The caller chuckled at his own wit.

"Don't be too sure of that. Look, let me take a guess. When you've driving around with Durango, what you'd like is to have him sit up and look around and generally behave like a guard dog. But he doesn't. He curls up and goes to sleep. Is that right?"

"Yeah, but it ain't only that. It's everything."

"He's friendly."

"Yeah."

"He doesn't threaten people. He acts sweet."

"Yuh, the big dope. That's what he is. He's a big dope."

"Let's not leap to conclusions here," I said. "Have you ever heard the term *alpha male*?" After a moment of silence, I explained. "In packs of wolves and dogs, the alpha male is the top-ranking animal of the pack, okay? And the true alpha, the established leader who knows he's top dog, is a calm, self-confident animal. What he doesn't do is go around snarling at everybody else or starting trouble or picking fights. Why should he? Everyone else already respects him. He's not some wannabe little scrapper. He's the boss."

"You don't know Durango."

Inspiration struck. "I do know Mr. Guarini," I said. "Do you ever see him going around getting in stupid little fights with everyone?"

"Mr. G.'s got a smile for everyone. Most of the time."

"Exactly. Does Mr. Guarini ride around in his car glaring out the window and baring his teeth at people and snarling? No. He relaxes. So does Durango. Durango is a self-confident alpha leader. Top dog. There is nothing wrong with him, and you can stop worrying." Wondering whether I was going a bit too far, I nonetheless added, "In fact, you can take pride in Durango. He sounds to me like the Enzio Guarini of dogs."

"You think so?"

"I'm positive," I lied. "I'm sure that if the need ever arises, Durango will show his strength. In the meantime, enjoy him. He sounds like a good dog."

I expected the caller to end the consultation there. He didn't. After a little um-ing and er-ing, he said in a reluctant tone, "Mr. G. says I gotta cut his balls off."

"Durango's, I presume." No, I didn't say it aloud. What I said was, "Mr. Guarini knows a lot about dogs. And, uh, analogies, uh, comparisons aside, dogs are, after all, dogs. Durango won't hold it against you. In fact, he'll never know. So, yes, you should do what Mr. Guarini tells you to do."

Purely by chance, the second little incident, another phone call, also occurred when I happened to be working with dogs. Do we detect a pattern here? Actually, I was training only one dog, Kimi, but my focus was again on aggression. Specifically, Kimi was learning to be a good girl in the presence of *our* cat, Tracker, and by *our*, as I was determined to convince Kimi, I meant hers, mine, and Rowdy's. The only way to ensure that a dog will be safe around cats is to raise the dog with cats from puppyhood. It also helps to start with a mild dog of a nonpredatory breed, meaning neither Kimi nor Rowdy nor any other malamute who hasn't grown up with cats. Tracker was a permanent resident of our household because, having rescued her, I'd failed to find any responsible person who was even remotely interested in adopting her. If you ignored Tracker's head, she was an attractive-enough-looking black cat, but she was missing a chunk of one ear, and a squiggly pink mark disfigured her face. Worse, her typical expression was sour, and she was fond of hissing at people. To protect her from the dogs, I kept her in my office, and I have to say that she was a nasty officemate. Whenever I wanted to use my computer and had to dislodge Tracker from the mousepad, she spat at me and often scratched my hands. Still, as I had to work at reminding myself, Tracker was not only one of God's creatures but *my* cat, and in confining her to one small room, I wasn't offering her an enviable existence. Also, it galled me to admit even to myself that I was incapable of teaching the dogs to accept her.

At the moment, Tracker was on top of the refrigerator, where she was going to linger because I'd supplied her with a plateful of Kitty Kaviar, which is shaved bonito and Tracker's favorite treat. Rowdy was safely locked in my bedroom, and Kimi was on a loose leash and wearing a snug fabric muzzle that allowed her to eat the morsels of roast beef I was giving her when I caught her displaying calm behavior toward Tracker. In the old days, we tried to catch our dogs doing something wrong so we could correct the behavior, usually by jerking on a choke chain. Now, we're equally vigilant in watching for good behavior, which we reward with positive reinforcement. I was using the same method I'd been teaching to Enzio Guarini, what's popularly called "clicker training" and technically known as "operant conditioning with an event marker." The event marker—the click—came from the little plastic and metal clicker I held in my hand. Each time Kimi glanced at Tracker without stiffening her legs, raising her hackles, or showing any other sign of excitement, I sounded the clicker and immediately followed the click with a treat. Just when I'd seen Kimi display a new and welcome behavior, the damned phone rang. For the first time, Kimi had calmly looked up at Tracker and then immediately turned her eyes to me in clear expectation of the click and treat, both which I delivered.

"Yes!" I told her. "That's it! You've got it!"

Oh, well, any good trainer knows to end a session on a note of success. I hustled Kimi into the bathroom, removed her muzzle, shut her in, and ran for the phone. I'm diligent about answering because I'm on many lists of volunteers for Alaskan Malamute Rescue of New England and the Alaskan Malamute Assistance League. The call I don't answer could be from someone who abandons the effort to reach Malamute Rescue and dumps some poor malamute at a kill shelter instead. Or worse.

This particular call had nothing to do with malamutes. It was another referral from Enzio Guarini. Like the call about Durango, this was a complaint about insufficient machismo, and before I get precise, I have to tell you that as a dog trainer, a dog writer, and especially as a volunteer for Malamute Rescue, I've dealt with thousands of dog problems. When my caller is someone new to malamutes, I often have to do nothing more than provide information. A typical such call goes like this:

New adopter of adult female malamute: Nikki's so sweet and wonderful, and we love her so much, but we're worried sick that there's something terribly wrong with her, uh, hormones.

Me: She lifts her leg.

Caller: Yes!

Me: That's perfectly normal.

If the dog is destroying the house, my advice is to increase the amount of exercise he gets and to stop giving him the run of the house. He jumps on people? Teach him a solid down-stay. And so forth. But with dog owners, just when you think you've heard it all, you learn better. Incredibly, incredibly, this caller was consulting me, a dog *trainer*, a specialist in *behavior*, because of his male rottweiler's infuriatingly disobedient refusal to grow to the gigantic size the owner wanted.

"My brother's got a rottweiler that weighs a hundred and seventy pounds," he informed me.

"Your brother's dog is too big," I said. "The rottweiler isn't supposed to be a giant breed. Your brother's dog is incorrect. And at a guess, he's fat. That dog would be laughed out of the show ring. The owner of the *correct* rottweiler is you."

For all I knew, my caller's "correct" rottie was thirty pounds overweight and a total fright. Did I care? I did not. My caller was delighted with what I'd told him. And my caller was a Guarini associate.

The third call came from Carla Cortiniglia, Joey's widow, and inevitably concerned her memorable little coffin-dancing, bosom-nestling loudmouth, Anthony. Carla began by repeating the profuse thanks she'd offered me at the funeral. "Geez, first Joey, and then if it would've been Anthony, too, I don't know what I would've done."

At worst, the undertakers would have raised Joey and then somehow raised Anthony from the ground; the rescue would have threatened the dignity of the service, but the dog's life hadn't been in any great danger.

I said, "I was glad to help."

"Anthony's got a mind of his own. He won't listen to

a word I say." Carla's proud tone was one that's dreaded by every sensible dog trainer.

I spoke honestly. "I have the feeling that you like Anthony just the way he is."

"I'm nuts about Anthony. You got that right! He walks all over me. But I really gotta do something."

"Dog trainers have a saying: If it's not a problem for *you*, it's not a problem. In other words, Anthony is your dog, and if you're happy with his behavior, that's what counts. Unless your neighbors are upset about something? Or he's biting people? Or—"

"I got a problem in my flower shop," Carla said. "It's my dream, you know? A flower shop. And as soon as I says to Enzio, 'Enzio, what am I gonna do without Joey?' he says to me, 'Carla, what do you wanna do?' and I says, 'Run a flower shop.' And he says, 'Well then Carla, that's what you're gonna do. Which one you want?' He's a good man. And I says, 'You know that one in the center of Munford? Just got redone, all clean and pretty? That's the kind of place I got in mind. That's my dream.' And you know what? The next day, Enzio calls me and he says, 'Carla? Your dream's come true.' "

My first thought, duh, was what an amazing coincidence it had been that the flower shop of Carla's dreams had just so happened to be for sale. My second thought was that whatever Enzio Guarini ever wanted would become instantly available. "And Anthony?" I asked.

"You gotta understand that Anthony, he's with me all the time. Like they say, twenty-four seven. He's my constant companion."

"Bosom companion," I blurted out. "Is that a problem?"

"I'm not leaving him home."

"Is there some reason why you should?"

There was. Anthony was ferociously guarding his new daytime home against the intruders who persistently tried to enter it. He was also attacking the stock: knocking over potted plants, ripping into ribbons, and puncturing Mylar balloons.

"For a dog," I lectured, "having free run of the house or the shop or anyplace else is a great privilege. And it's a privilege that has to be earned. Anthony has not earned the privilege. And I'm sorry to say that he's going to have to have the privilege taken away until he does earn it, or you are going to have no customers and nothing to sell them, anyway."

"He's being just awful," Carla said.

It's important to instill hope. "Anthony could be an asset to your business," I said. "He's very cute. The problem isn't *Anthony*." Naturally I was tempted to say, "It's *you*." I didn't. "The problem is Anthony's *behavior*. That's an important distinction. You love Anthony. And what he needs right now is tough love. We can work on his behavior, but it's going to be hard work, and he's not going to shape up instantly. Okay? Carla, do you own a crate?"

"I'm not putting Anthony in a cage!"

"If you let him keep doing what he's doing, you're letting him practice undesirable behavior. All these behaviors are becoming habits, and once a behavior becomes habitual, and it's locked in, it's almost impossible to change." Yes, as in *habitual* criminal. It seemed to me that I'd do well to say no more.

"I saw what you did with Anthony. It was a miracle. Could you come over here?" Carla pleaded.

"Yes. But not now." I love training dogs, and I love teaching people to train dogs. What Carla wanted wasn't what I had to offer; as she'd just said, she wanted a miracle and, worse yet, a miracle performed by me. Of course, a miracle was what I wanted, too: I wanted Carla to undergo a personality transplant that would replace her hysteria with someone else's calm realism. Then I could help her to train her dog.

"Tomorrow?" she asked.

"Carla, I just can't." I went on to offer an excuse, possibly the only one that Enzio Guarini would fully accept. "Both of my dogs are entered in a show on Saturday. Tomorrow, I absolutely have to bathe and groom them. Your shop isn't open on Sunday, is it?"

"No, but—"

"Monday," I said. "I'll be there Monday morning."

She gave me directions. I gave her the toll-free number of a mail-order kennel-supply house and issued a dog trainer's do-it-now command to buy a dog crate.

Carla promised to order the crate immediately. I had convinced a mafioso's widow to lock up her dog—or, as Carla phrased it, to put poor, dear, innocent baby Anthony in jail. You see? I really did perform a miracle. Or so I thought at the time.

CHAPTER 12

So, here we are—my cousin Leah, my friend Mary Wood, and I—and it's Saturday at what feels like four o'clock in the morning, but is actually a bit after dawn. Although we've been up for hours and are perfectly used to refusing the pleas of beds that beg us to linger, we're nonetheless a little puffy eyed and a lot overcaffeinated. But who cares about *us*? We're mere human beings, and this is dog show! The creatures who matter are Rowdy and Kimi and Mr. Wookie, and they're bright-eyed and eager and gorgeous. And, well they should be having fun because they're not the ones lugging grooming tables, tack boxes, and Vari-Kennels out of my disreputable Bronco and Mary's spiffy rental van, are they? The dogs aren't swearing. Far from it. Mr. Wookie, in particular, is addressing Mary in what resemble animated English sentences minus only the trivia of identifiable words. I'm the one who's cursing, and the reason is that I've just discovered that the worn spot on the floor behind the driver's seat of my car has become a hole through which I can see blacktop.

Mr. Wookie has as much reason to voice joyful self-confidence about his chances in the ring as I do to mutter obscenities about my car. Indeed, I share Mr. Wookie's expectations. Harry Howland, our judge, has never yet overlooked this stunning seal-and-white boy. "Seal" means a black guard coat over a light undercoat. Mr. Wookie is thus dark and handsome, elegantly reminiscent of a high-society gentleman in a tuxedo. He's exactly as tall as he's supposed to be, twenty five and three-eighths inches at the withers, to be precise, the withers being the highest point of the back, where the neck begins, above the forelegs. He is a superbly correct malamute and a superb showman. A single hair from Mr. Wookie's undercoat has enough vibrant personality for a thousand ordinary dogs. Lest I sound disloyal to Rowdy, let me state the obvious: My own boy is himself no ordinary dog and no ordinary show dog, and even under Harry Howland, Rowdy might give Mr. Wookie some serious competition. Rowdy, too, is all a malamute should be, and he, too, is a show-offy show dog. Today, however, he is at a great disadvantage. The disadvantage is named Holly Winter. Mr. Wookie is always owner-handled by Mary, who is slim, pretty, and feminine, the perfect foil for her ruggedly handsome dog. What Mary and Mr. Wookie share, however, besides the superficial trait of dark hair, is an attitude toward life in general and dog shows in particular that's outgoing, friendly, likeable, and contagious. They both talk a lot, especially to each other. Their rapport in the ring is legendary.

As usual, Mr. Wookie will be owner-handled today. As is anything but usual, and for good reason, it looks as though Rowdy, too, may be owner-handled. In the short time since we arrived in the parking lot, five people with cell phones have come running up to me with the same message from Faith Barlow, Rowdy's handler, who wants me to know that in the middle of the night, she tripped over a dog toy, landed in a whelping box, and broke her left arm. Faith is still stuck at the hospital and has been unable to find me a substitute handler.

"Handle him yourself," says Mary.

"I am a dreadful breed handler," I say. *Breed,* I should mention, is conformation, the *show* part of a dog show, the competition succinctly, if incorrectly, described as a beauty contest. "Ask Leah!"

"She's terrible," says my cousin, who must be believed because she's a Harvard undergraduate and therefore knows everything. "Her hands shake." Although Leah does not look her best at this ghastly hour, she is still strikingly lovely. Her best is spectacular. She has masses of red-gold curls and looks altogether like an anomalously athletic and all-American version of those otherworldly young women depicted in the paintings of Burne-Jones. She enunciates clearly and has an authoritative, educated voice that carries with hideous effectiveness even when she whispers. "Holly hates handling breed," she says. "It makes her throw up."

"The risk," I say truthfully, "isn't vomiting. It's fainting."

Mary laughs off the truth. "Holly, you handle in obedience! In breed, Rowdy can practically show himself."

As I didn't bother to say, almost no one uses a professional handler in obedience. Besides, with malamutes, it's hard enough to get the dog to obey *you*, never mind someone else. As to Rowdy, considering his history of hijinks in the obedience ring, if he weren't my dog, I wouldn't handle him in so-called obedience for a million dollars. Leah handled Kimi in both breed and obedience. That's Harvard for you: omnicompetence all over.

"Leah," I say with happy inspiration, "maybe Harry Howland won't look twice at Kimi, and you can take Rowdy in."

If I start explaining all about the judging of dog shows, we'll never get back to Joey Cortiniglia and the Mob, so let me just say that Kimi was entered in a class of female malamutes ("Open Bitches") who were competing for championship points, whereas Rowdy and Mr. Wookie had already finished their championships and wouldn't enter the ring until the last part of the malamute judging, Best of Breed. Judging is a process of selective elimination. The judge starts with the dog classes and then does the bitch classes and finally does Best of Breed. Consequently, if today's malamute judge, Harry Howland, failed to appreciate Kimi when he judged Open Bitches, Kimi would be eliminated from further competition for the day. In that case, Leah would be available to handle Rowdy in Best of Breed. And I wouldn't have to.

"Leah," says Mary, glaring at me, "Harry Howland's going to love Kimi. Don't listen to Holly. You're going to go in there and win. Holly's going to have to find someone else for Rowdy or take him in herself, because you're going to be back in the ring."

"I'll find someone," I say. In fact, I've already asked all the people who've relayed Faith's messages, and I've had no luck at all.

As we head across the blacktop toward the trade center that serves as the show site, Mary is quietly taking me to task for expressing a discouraging attitude to Leah and Kimi, and somewhat less quietly is asking me whether I really throw up or faint in the ring. I'm feeling guilty about my negative attitude and change the topic by grumbling loudly about the hole in the floor of my car and my desire to have the wreck vaporize, when all of a sudden I'm startled by a lugubrious, adenoidal male voice that says, "You want some help?"

To my embarrassment, the speaker is the mafioso Dracula himself, Al Favuzza, and with him are scrawny, greasy little Zap the Driver and the hulking monster-twin corpse movers. Committed as I am to the abhorrent policy of making nice to the Mob until I can sever my connection, I resist the urge to tell Favuzza to climb back into his coffin. As I'm trying to dream up an alternative greeting, I nod to Al, Zap, and the twins, and Mary, who's noticed my nod of recognition, says, "Thanks. We'd love some help." As I've said, that's Mary: friendly. Also, intelligent. Why should we haul all this gear when we can get someone else to do it? She goes on to introduce herself. "I'm Mary Wood." She smiles. So does Leah, who says, "I'm Leah Whitcomb, Holly's cousin."

To my horror, Favuzza's eyes are fixed on Leah: the masses of curls, the voluptuousness that accentuates the baby-perfection of her fair skin. I struggle to collect myself. For all that Mary and Leah know, the mobsters are purebred dogsters of an admittedly thuggish sort. After a glance at the young, old, fat, skinny, garish, conservative, noisy, and silent exhibitors making their way toward the trade center with their giant, toy, hairy, hairless, brawny, bony, yappy, and barkless dogs, I see that what marks the members of the dog fancy as such is nothing more complicated than animation: Our eyes are alive. By comparison, Guarini's henchmen are the living dead.

A benign explanation for the mobsters' presence finally occurs to me: Guarini's underlings are an advance force charged with the job of checking out the show before the boss arrives. Specifically, they're on the lookout for another dog lover, namely, Blackie Lanigan.

"Is Mr. Guarini coming?" I ask brightly.

Favuzza's eyes move from Leah to me and back again. If you looked in the seafood case at a market and saw a fish with eyes like that, you wouldn't buy it. "No," he says.

As we enter the trade center, I'm hoping that the hoodlums will be told that this entrance is for exhibitors only and that spectators are required to use a different entrance, preferably one located ten thousand miles away. As it is,

Mary, Leah, and I show our entry forms, the gangsters pay to enter, and all of us get the backs of our hands stamped in purple ink. Zap humiliates me by refusing to hold out his grubby hands for the rubber stamp, but the gargantuan twins surround him, and Favuzza says, "So's you can go out and go back in without paying, you moron."

Although we've arrived early, the exhibition hall gives off the rich mix of odors that define a dog show, the fragrances of grooming spray, liver treats, cedar shavings, women's perfume, men's cologne, nervous human sweat, premium dog food, soggy sandwiches, stale doughnuts, burned coffee, and hot competition. The grooming area is conveniently near the entrance. It's already lined with rows of crates, coolers, folding chairs, and grooming tables. Underfoot are heavy-duty extension cords. Here and there, patterned area rugs add a homey touch. Trailed by our mobster helpers, Mary, Leah, and I find space to set up. As one of the monstrous twins effortlessly lifts my heavy grooming table, I can't help thinking of the millions of times my muscles have screamed under the weight of the damned thing. My conscience may object to racketeer assistance, but my body is grateful. Still, now that Al, Zap, and the big-lug twins have finished providing the help they offered, I'm hoping they'll depart, but out of nowhere, Leah turns to Favuzza and says, "I know where I met you! At the Museum of Fine Arts."

I think, but don't say, "Oh, sure. Or was it at Symphony Hall?"

Leah adds, "You asked me for directions. I knew I'd met you before."

Favuzza makes a squeaky grunt. The merest hint of something resembling human feeling crosses his face, but it passes so swiftly that I cannot begin to guess what emotion, if any, it reflects.

"Kimi, table!" Leah says, and my lovely Kimi leaps and plants her four big paws on the rubber-matted surface, wags her tail, and looks around to make sure that people are watching her. No one is. The other exhibitors are socializing with one another and working on their dogs. Mary now has Mr. Wookie up on the table she has borrowed from me. Mary and Leah are both wearing white lab coats over the dressy clothes that are de rigueur in the conformation ring. Al Favuzza is ogling Leah. Zap is staring at Mr. Wookie, who is so eye catching that he'd be used to stares if he were just a family pet who got routinely walked around the block. As it is, he's an experienced player in the dog show game and understands that drawing attention to himself is an essential move. Watching Zap watching Mr. Wookie, I just know what's coming next. Before I can forestall it, Zap sidles up to Mary and says, "How much you want for him?"

Mr. Wookie is BISS International/American CH Malko's Wookie of Kunek, WPD, CGC. Mary is used to people who fail to realize that he is *her* dog. When they aren't asking to buy him, they're informing her that they're going to use him at stud. Hah! No one breathes near Mr. Wookie without Mary's consent.

Belatedly, I say to Zap, "Mary is very definitely not

interested in selling him, and it happens to be against the rules of the American Kennel club to buy or sell a dog at a show."

"Zap, you moron," Favuzza says, "the boss told you that, and he told you to shut up, so shut up."

Enzio Guarini has instructed Zap on dog show etiquette? Why? What are these horrible men doing here? The only answer that comes to mind is: embarrassing me.

My watch reads 8:30. Malamute judging is scheduled for 9:00 in Ring 7. My brain is bouncing up and down, and turning somersaults trying to think up a way to ditch Guarini's men. I know a lot of people in dogs, I know everyone in malamutes, and I do not want to be seen with this entourage of goons.

"How'd you like to do me a favor?" I ask Zap. "Could you go buy me a show catalog?" And to the massive twins, I say, "I could sure use some coffee, and Mary and Leah could, too." I'm starting to hand out money, but Favuzza stops me by saying it's all his treat. What I'm hoping in assigning the errands is that Zap and the twins will get lost and won't find us again until the judging is over. Zap and the twins depart. Three thugs down, one to go. Also, of course, I need to find a handler for Rowdy. But before I can concoct a mission for Favuzza, he draws me aside and says, "I hear you got a problem today."

Blood rushes to my face as I think, "Yes, you!" Blood. How appropriate! I sneak a glance at his teeth to see whether his canines are elongating. "No, no problem at all, certainly not, everything's just fine, it's wonderful. Things could not be better except that my car has a hole in the floor, and I wish the damned thing would vaporize, and I've got to find someone to take Rowdy for me. His handler broke her arm, and if I don't find someone else, I'll have to take him in the ring myself, and I'm not even dressed for it."

The American Kennel Club expects handlers to be properly attired. Men wear suits or sport coats. Women wear dresses or pants outfits. For once, I'm not in jeans and a T-shirt, but my navy cords and white cotton sweater are too informal for the breed ring. Beneath Mary's lab coat is a black dress that matches her dog's dark coat. The red-piped jacket that goes with the dress is in a dry cleaner's bag on top of Mr. Wookie's crate. Leah has on a white silk blouse and a short navy blue pleated skirt. Her red blazer will remain in its plastic bag until the last minute. Out of the corner of my eye, I catch sight of two professional handlers, Derek Slate and Rob Leist, and I dash after them, but neither is free to handle Rowdy, and neither knows anyone who is. I return to find that Leah, bless her, has Rowdy on the table and is spritzing him with water and fluffing him with a Mason-Pearson brush and a powerful stream of air from our dryer. Mary, meanwhile, is misting Mr. Wookie with water and touching up his already perfect coat with a metal comb.

Eager for a few grooming tips, are you? I'd spill all the secrets, but sooner or later I'd still have to get to the matter of my moral compromise. I am deeply ashamed to have had any part in what happened in the ring. I accept full responsibility. I am heartily sorry.

CHAPTER 13

That day's malamute judge, Harry Howland, was the head of a family business that manufactured and distributed the kinds of cardboard containers used for take-out pizza and pastry. Ironically, it's possible that Harry Howland's company was the very one that had made the pastry box containing Enzio Guarini's Kimi-filched cannoli. But for once, these so-called coincidences (*dog* spelled backward) are irrelevant. What you need to know about Harry Howland is, first, that he was an AKC judge and, second, that he knew my father and had known my late mother, who bred top-winning golden retrievers and was a Power in the Dog Fancy. In case you don't show dogs, let me briefly explain that the American Kennel Club not only expects its judges to be treated with the utmost in courtesy and respect, but with the goal of seeing these

happy expectations fulfilled, publishes disciplinary guidelines that spell out the nasty consequences of displaying
rudeness, disrespect, or worse toward an AKC judge. For example, aggravated physical abuse of a judge can get you a
fine of $5,000 and the suspension of AKC privileges for ten
years. More to the point—the point toward which we are,
alas, heading—the offense of attempting to influence a
judge carries a standard penalty of a $500 fine and an 18-
month suspension of privileges. Suspension of AKC privileges: For the duration, you can't show a dog or do much else
that counts in life, especially in my life. As to Harry Howland's acquaintance with my parents, Mr. Howland . . .
well, we're about to get to that.

But let's start at the beginning of Harry Howland's
judging of my breed, the Alaskan malamute, which took
place as scheduled in Ring 7 and was about to begin only
about ten minutes late, which is to say, at about 9:10.
Within the sacred precincts of the baby-gated ring, Harry
Howland and his stewards were busy with paperwork, and
at the judge's table, a few handlers were still picking up
armbands. Harry Howland was a tall, silver-haired man
of distinguished appearance who so thoroughly looked the
part of an AKC judge that his photograph appeared in
educational materials about the judging of dog shows distributed by the AKC. I did not look distinguished. Having failed to find someone else to handle Rowdy for me,
I'd not only picked up his armband, but fastened it on
my left upper arm over the sleeve of my red blazer, which
was actually Leah's. In a doomed effort to look properly
dressed, I'd convinced her that she'd be fine in her white

silk blouse and navy-blue pleated skirt and that I needed the blazer more than she did. "You hate red," I'd pointed out. "You never wear it. You think it looks awful with your hair."

"It looks beautiful with her hair," Mary had said.

"True," I'd said. "But Leah doesn't think so."

I'd brushed my hair, applied blush and lipstick, donned the blazer, and reconciled myself to handling Rowdy myself if my ringside efforts to find a handler failed, as they had. As to the armband, maybe I need to note the sportsmanlike fiction that the judge has no idea of the identities of dogs and handlers, each dog being identified only by the number on the handler's armband and the judge being prohibited from looking at the show catalog, which publishes the names of the dogs together with their corresponding numbers. In reality, even as small worlds go, this one is minuscule. Judges recognize dogs and handlers because they've seen them everywhere, in the ring and in ads in dog magazines.

Now, as Leah, Kimi, Mary, Mr. Wookie, Rowdy, and I stood outside Ring 7 with a lot of other handlers and malamutes, as well as a small crowd of spectators, I said, mainly to myself, "After all, I *am* an experienced handler. What's the worst that can happen?"

Leah said, "You could faint or throw up."

"I'm not woozy, and my stomach is okay."

Leah continued. "Rowdy could get in a fight, or you could trip and fall on your face."

"The two of you!" Mary was misting Mr. Wookie's coat and fluffing him up here and there with a small pin brush

that bore his portrait on the back. Mr. Wookie was voicing a highly inflected opinion. Although his vocalizations
sounded strangely like the word *no,* he was clearly expressing his ardent desire to get in the ring and win:
"Let's go!"

As Mary was replying to Mr. Wookie, I glanced at the
judge's table and saw to my horror that Harry Howland
was standing by the gate in conversation with—oh no!—
Al Favuzza. Having dispatched the horrible twins and
Zap the Driver on errands, I'd finally rid us of Favuzza
by sending him off to buy a new show lead. Show leads
are thin leashes that come in a zillion styles and materials.
The nylon ones are available in dozens of colors. With
luck, I'd thought, the vampire would linger over a be-
wildering display and then be unable to find us because
we'd have moved from the grooming area to ringside.
Hah! Here he was. Worse, here he was talking to Harry
Howland.

Noting Favuzza, Leah said, "He's probably asking
where we are. He wouldn't know not to do that. You
know, Holly, when I saw him at the Museum of Fine
Arts, it was just so sad. He didn't actually ask me for
directions. He asked me how to get in, and finally I realized that he didn't know that all he had to do was walk
in and pay. Can you imagine a person who doesn't realize
that the museum is open to the public? It's terrible that
anyone would feel so disenfranchised."

"Disenfranchised!" I didn't share Leah's egalitarian interpretation. Favuzza was probably planning to rob the

museum. "Leah," I said, "I don't like the way he looks at you. Stay away from him."

She laughed. "That's ridiculous! He's a middle-aged man. All of a sudden, you're a paranoid snob?"

"I am *not* a snob, and I am *not* paranoid." Fleeing the repulsive image of Leah as the object of Favuzza's interest, I changed the subject. "This is one of the puppy classes, right?"

Male puppies. As I've mentioned in passing, the judging of dog-show classes is not coed. The boys go first. I don't mind: I'm so used to the system that I expect to arrive at the Pearly Gates and hang around while St. Peter judges the men. Without doubt, I'll get there with a spray bottle of water in one hand and a brush in the other, and I'll mist my own hair and pretty it up just as I was now spritzing and stroking Rowdy's coat. The entry will presumably be larger than today's malamute entry, which, although small, was decent for our part of the country. The total number of malamutes entered was twenty-two, with ten in the dog classes, seven in the bitch classes, and the remainder, including Rowdy and Mr. Wookie, in Best of Breed. It was unlikely that everyone would show up.

Unfortunately, the people who showed up in my immediate vicinity were not malamute exhibitors, but the entire crew of mobsters, led by Al Favuzza, who said, "What are you waiting for?" Favuzza's line of work, I thought, had left him sadly unable to delay gratification.

"My turn," I said. "The ones in the ring now are class dogs, meaning that they aren't champions. They're competing for championship points. Rowdy's finished. He has to wait until after the class dogs and then the class bitches are judged. Then there'll be a sort of grand finale, with the winners from the classes—and the champions. The judge picks his Best of Breed, Best of Opposite Sex, and Best of Winners, which could be . . . well, let's just say that at the moment we're waiting for Kimi's turn."

In case it seems as if I've disparaged AKC judges with my talk about the polite fiction of numbered armbands and so on, let me say that judging is hard work. AKC judges have to follow a prescribed protocol, do their AKC paperwork correctly, and keep to a schedule that allots only a few minutes to evaluate each dog. New judges are expected to do twenty dogs per hour; experienced judges, twenty-five. Harry Howland was experienced. And he was good: He was paying attention to every dog while simultaneously moving the judging along in an appropriately efficient manner. Also, his first-place winner in Open Dogs, who also went Winners Dog, was the one I'd've picked myself.

Then he started on the bitches. The one puppy entered was a no-show, and the single Bred-by-Exhibitor bitch obviously had no trouble winning her class. As Leah, Kimi, and the others entered in Open Bitches filed into the ring, one bitch passed close to Mr. Wookie, who for once turned his attention from Mary and showed every intention of following the fetching femme instead. "No girls!" Mary told him. Meanwhile, Favuzza was ogling Leah so disgustingly that I almost issued the same order to him: "No girls!"

As to the malamute girls in the ring, one of Kimi's
competitors struck me as no competition. She had a sni-
pey muzzle, big ears, and a tight tail, and when she
moved, her extra flesh jiggled like Jell-O. Of the remain-
ing three, one was probably going to lose for an unfair
reason: She was red. Here in New England, we see very
few reds. According to the AKC standard of the breed,
color counts for nothing; it's strictly a matter of personal
preference. Still, most judges hesitate to put up a dog
that looks radically different from the others in the ring.
The other two were gray and white. Both were lighter
than Kimi and, in contrast to Kimi, they had "open faces"
like Rowdy's, all white, without bars, goggles, or other
markings. In malamutes, markings are supposed to be
symmetric. Otherwise, like color, they're nothing more
than interesting variations in a variable breed. What *does*
count? *Type:* Malamutes should look like malamutes, not
like Siberian huskies, collies, or akitas, for example. *Sound-
ness:* Malamutes should be built to move heavy loads over
great and bitterly cold distances. One of the two light
gray bitches was, to my eye, delicately pretty, not to mention cow-hocked, but her professional handler, Johnny Lamotte, was a wizard. Lamotte could get correct movement
from a dog with no legs, so this bitch's gait looked at
least passable. That's better than I can say about the second light gray bitch, who moved by flinging her hind
legs skyward. The hindquarters are supposed to drive the
dog efficiently forward; it's a waste of energy to treat the
heavens to a prolonged view of the pads of the feet. Kimi,
in contrast, moved beautifully. Furthermore, Leah han-

dled her well. Together, Kimi and Leah created a winning
picture. And won the class. As I've said, Harry Howland
is a *good* judge.

As he handed out the ribbons, Mary joined in the ap-
plause. I did, too, of course. Favuzza, Zap, and the twin
thugs didn't. Barbarians! Worse, Favuzza jerked his thumb
toward the ring in an apparent effort to tell me to get
Rowdy in there. As if *I* needed direction at a dog show!

"Not quite yet," I said. "Now the winners from the
bitch classes, the first-place bitches, go back in again."

That's what they were doing, of course. The class is
called Winners, and—surprise!—the victor is called Winners Bitch. She and the Winners Dog are the ones who
get the championship points. With the wisdom born of
experience, the AKC recognizes that snafus occur.
Therefore, the judge also selects an RWD and an RWB,
reserve winners, the dog and the bitch who earn the
points if the WD or the WB is "disallowed," as it's said.

"Kimi's my Reserve Queen." I said to Mary. "I could
wallpaper a room in purple and white ribbons. People
keep telling me to hire a handler, but I really want Leah
to be able to finish Kimi herself."

"She's going to win," Mary said. "Howland loves her.
I can tell."

Mary was right. Just as I'd taught her, Leah, having
accepted the ribbon, was speaking politely to everyone
else in the ring instead of rudely ignoring the other handlers while leaping up and down in obnoxious celebration
of the win.

I nervously ran the brush over Rowdy and joined the dogs and handlers lining up for Best of Breed. Rowdy would be competing against Kimi, as well as against the Winners Dog and against the other specials, including Mr. Wookie. As I entered the ring, Harry Howland's eyes met mine. In this situation, even if the judge is an old family friend, he's a judge first: Harry Howland wouldn't stroll up to me to spend twenty minutes chitchatting about how my father was doing and how I liked my new stepmother. On the other hand, nothing in the AKC regulations or guidelines prevented him from wearing a pleasant expression, and absolutely nothing required him to glare at me and grit his teeth. Instead of focusing on Rowdy, I looked down at Leah's red blazer and my way-too-informal pants. Just ahead of me, the professional handler of an oversized, ponderous dog slowed way down. Fortunately, I caught the change of pace in time to avoid running Rowdy into the dog.

After that, I paid attention. Rowdy free-stacks well. I let him pose himself. My tension was already traveling down his show lead, and my trembling hands would've given him an alarm message if I'd fussed around in an effort to improve on perfection. But I did bait Rowdy. *Bait:* show verb meaning to induce the dog to look his animated best by offering a delectable incentive such as liver, beef, chicken, or Mr. Wookie's favorite, beef-flavored Redbarn roll. My own dogs will bait for dirt, but as the—ahem!—soon-to-be-esteemed author of the soon-to-be-published volume entitled *101 Ways to Cook Liver*, I had a freezer full of guess what and was using it. To reiterate, I knew we wouldn't win. So why bother trying? Pride. The malamute community was my community, and its members were people whose good opinions I valued. Win or lose, Rowdy was going to look good and show well.

Rowdy did his part. When Harry Howland ran his hands over Rowdy, there wasn't a growl or a grumble. As perhaps you know, these examinations are quite intimate because the judge has to check for the presence of the two required testicles. A rough judge can teach a dog to hate the show ring. Howland was respectful. Furthermore, when he checked Rowdy's bite, he had me open Rowdy's mouth. I just hate it when judges insist on transmitting microorganisms by sticking their increasingly germy hands into the mouths of all the dogs. So, Howland treated Rowdy with consideration. As to his treatment of me, he didn't grab and squeeze any sensitive body parts or shove his fingers in my throat, but his frozen face suggested that pain and disease were what I deserved. For failing to be Ms. Dog Show Fashion Plate?

Hurt and mystified, I did a bad job of gaiting Rowdy. My balance felt off. If the mats had been in poor condition, I'd probably have tripped and fallen. After that, I pulled myself together and concentrated on keeping Rowdy happy. He'd done nothing wrong, and I made sure he felt good about himself by doling out liver and sweet talk. When Harry Howland gave Mr. Wookie Best of Breed, I clapped with genuine enthusiasm, and when my lovely Kimi took Best of Winners and Best of Opposite— Best of Opposite Sex to Best of Breed—I was so thrilled

for her and for Leah that I momentarily quit wondering
what I'd done to offend the judge. Rowdy and I left the
ring. In it, Leah was busy hugging Mary and exchanging
congratulations, accepting congratulations from other handlers, and in general behaving like the modest, gracious
winner she was.

From inside the ring, Mary waved to me and called
out, "See? I told you! Cream always rises to the top!"

The show photographer was already in the ring. Concerned that Leah might try to spare me the expense of a
photo, I went through the gate and started toward Leah
to authorize the expenditure. Before I reached her, Harry
Howland approached me and silently motioned me aside.
It's common for judges to hand out advice: *Take handling
classes* or *Get someone to teach you to groom your dog.* I wasn't
worried. On the contrary, I felt relieved that I'd finally
get a full explanation for Harry's uncharacteristic coldness
toward me. I expected to be taken to task for dressing in
a manner disrespectful to the Sport, with a capital S.
What else had I done? Or failed to do?

I anticipated the justifiable criticism of my attire by
saying, "My handler broke her arm this morning. I didn't
expect to be in the ring. That's why I'm dressed like this.
I'm very sorry. It won't happen again."

Harry made one of those sounds on which silver-haired
gentlemen seem to hold a monopoly, a sort of baffled,
dismissive snort. "There's one reason I'm not reporting
you," he said, "and that's your mother. I do not want to
see Marissa Winter's daughter subjected to the public
censure you deserve."

For wearing corduroy pants instead of a skirt?

Harry Howland went on. "But if you should *ever* again attempt to influence me, I will see to it that you are raked over the coals, young lady." He paused for breath. His whole face was red, and the broken veins around his nose stood out. "Does your father know about these hoodlums of yours?"

I closed my eyes, opened them, and said, "Harry, I had no idea. None. There has been a horrible misunderstanding. I would never try to influence a judge. *Never.* I had no idea."

It was clear that Harry Howland didn't believe me. "By the way," he said, "it might interest you to know that my Best of Breed won strictly on his merits. I will not respond to threats—one way or the other. And another thing. Don't ever show a dog to me again as long as you live."

CHAPTER 1 4

Angry doesn't begin to say it. Nor does *mortified* Spotting Al Favuzza, Zap, and the twins outside a nearby ring, I hauled Rowdy over to them and spat out, "We need to talk, and we need to talk right now. Not here. Outside."

With the gang of gangsters trailing behind, I led Rowdy through the aisle to the exit, where I dutifully showed his entry form before hurrying through. Technically, the parking lot was on show grounds, but the ground outdoors felt less AKC-hallowed than did the interior of the trade center. The standard penalty for hollering at spectators ("Offense II, Disorderly Conduct, b. Abusive or foul language/verbal altercation") was a one-month suspension and a $500 fine, far milder than the punishment for attempting to influence a judge, but I didn't want to run any risks. We went all the way across the asphalt to a narrow, ugly strip of weeds bordering a rusty chain-link fence.

"Angry doesn't begin to say it," I told Al Favuzza, clearly the leader of the pack as well as the one I'd seen speaking to Harry Howland. "This is unbelievable!" As if to illustrate my sentiment, Rowdy lifted his leg on the fence and emptied his full bladder. The deserving object wasn't the unobjectionable fence. It was Al Favuzza.

"Some people don't know what's good for 'em," Favuzza said.

"I know perfectly well what is and isn't good for me! I make my living in the world of dogs, and it's a damned small living as it is, and what I do *not* need is to lose my AKC privileges or pay a huge fine or have my reputation ruined forever, and I cannot imagine what you thought you were doing or why you thought you were doing it, but one thing I can tell you is that this is *never* going to happen again, because I won't allow it. I have never been so mortified in my entire life. Do you realize that I know just about every person who was in or near that ring today?" Abruptly changing my tone of voice, I said, "Rowdy. I am not yelling at you. You are a good boy."

"Hey," said Favuzza, "it's only a dog show."

"ONLY? ONLY? It's only a place where I know everyone and everyone knows me. I have been showing dogs since before I was born"—true, in utero—"and I intend to keep on showing dogs until I keel over in the ring, and when that happens, I would like it to happen because I've died of old age and not because I've died of embarrassment and humiliation and goddamned disbelief the way I practically did today."

Having been informed that he was not the subject of my tirade, Rowdy took an intelligent interest in it. That's more than can be said for Guarini's henchmen. Rowdy's beautiful almond-shaped eyes focused on me with fascination. In a canine enactment of *A Midsummer Night's Dream*, he'd've made a brilliant Puck: *What fools these mortals be!*

"Do you have something to say for yourselves?" I demanded. "If you're at a loss for words, you could start by apologizing."

To my surprise, it was Zap who replied. "Joey'd uh done a better job."

"Of what?" I tried to ask, but Favuzza drowned me out by saying, "Zap, shut up. Joey's dead. How could he've done a better job when he's dead?"

The horrible twins shuffled their feet and emitted subhuman grunts apparently intended to express approval of Favuzza's wit.

"Yeah, well," Favuzza continued, "there's more dog shows. Hey, kid gloves is always a big mistake, so let's forget about today. Next time it's all going to work out."

"Next time? *Next time?*" I was beside myself. "There is going to be no *next* time. All of a sudden, I see everything, okay? What we're having here is a series of miscommunications. I am not upset because Rowdy lost today. For one thing, he lost to a really good dog. It's no shame to lose to Mr. Wookie. And for another thing, anyone who can't stand to lose shouldn't be showing dogs at all because no one wins all the time, and I of all people know that, so what I'm upset about, what I'm, uh, practically speechless about, is that you saw fit to jeopardize my good standing in my sport and my friendship with Mary Wood and my goddamned honesty by threatening an American Kennel Club judge who just so happens to be someone I've known my entire life and who is forever after going to think I'm a sleaze and a cheat. And *that's* what I'm so-called *upset* about!"

"We were only trying to do you a favor," Favuzza said.

"A favor? By ruining my reputation? This is your idea of a favor?" After I spoke, it occurred to me that the botched gangland "favor" actually could have been worse than the one I was enduring. Everyone involved was still breathing. Notice that I did not ask what the favor was supposed to be for. Keeping my mouth shut about Joey Cortiniglia's murder?

Zap said, "For helping the boss."

In an effort to supply a benign explanation of why Guarini owed me a favor, I said, "With Frey."

"Because you won't take no money." Zap was on the verge of elaborating, but Favuzza, as usual, told him to shut up.

"That's a gift," I said. "If I wanted any kind of payment for it, I'd send a bill. And I want it clearly understood that my dogs and I win or lose on our own. When my dogs win, I want to know that they've won because they were the best. Period. And when they lose, all I want is to have a good time anyway."

"No dog favors," Favuzza said.

"Exactly. No dog favors. No dog favors ever again."

CHAPTER 1 5

No *dog* favors. Mistake. No *favors*. But that's not what I'd said.

The delivery was on my doorstep when Leah, Mary, and I, together with Kimi, Rowdy, and Mr. Wookie, got home from the show. In taking Best of Breed, Mr. Wookie had thereby become the Alaskan malamute's representative in the Working Group competition, an event that obviously could not be held until after the judging of all Working Group breeds—the akita, the Siberian husky, the Bernese mountain dog, the Samoyed, and so on—and thus took place near the end of the show day. You occasionally hear people maintain that they don't like having their dogs go BOB because the win necessitates hanging around all day for the group judging, which is to say that the Dog Fancy, like the rest of the world, has its share of liars. Mary was perfectly truthful about her pleasure at Mr. Wookie's win, and all of us were outright delighted when her beautiful dog took the Working Group. Best in Show, alas, went to a breed I shall refrain from specifying lest I create hard feeling among fanciers of the nasty-tempered canines known affectionately, or so Leah remarked, as "the breed for owners who don't have the guts to bite people themselves."

But Mary was nonetheless thrilled with Mr. Wookie's Group I, so when we got to my house and found the case of wine and the big box of restaurant-grade steak on the doorstep with my name on them, I had to let her think I'd ordered the supplies in confident expectation of the need to celebrate. Leah usually has better things to do on a Saturday night than hang out with the dogs and me, but the sight of all that food and wine made her hungry, thirsty, and generous. With my permission, she called one of her roommates to extend a dinner invitation that was not only accepted, but passed along. Meanwhile I'd run into Artie Spicer and Rita, and I'd invited the two of them. Furthermore, when Kevin Dennehy happened along while Mary was unloading her van (she was staying with me), I could hardly let him haul in all the dog gear and Mary's luggage, and then exclude him. By 8:30, Artie Spicer had my Weber grill going in the yard, and in my kitchen and living room were Mary, Rita, Kevin, Leah, and six or eight of Leah's undergraduate friends, all drinking delicious Italian wine.

"They're not driving," I told Lieutenant Kevin Dennehy of the Cambridge police, who said, "Driving? With me here, they're not even *drinking*. I don't see them drinking. Do you?"

"No, of course not." I was delighted to have Kevin's attention focused on the wine's illicit destination instead of its indubitably criminal source. In my innocence, I could only guess at how Guarini had arranged the delivery. Were the wine and beef stolen goods? Extortion payments? Kevin's guess would be better than mine. I didn't ask him. And everyone at my impromptu party was too polite to wonder aloud how an impoverished dog writer was paying for the feast. While Artie grilled the ill-gotten steaks, Rita raided her refrigerator and mine to put together a salad, and I transferred French bread from my freezer to the oven. The food was, I have to say, delicious. The party was a great success.

As if to demonstrate that dog people are capable of conversation on noncanine topics, Mary talked with Artie Spicer about birds. Artie belonged to numerous birding groups, subscribed to birding magazines, and sometimes contributed articles to them. Rita had met Artie when she'd joined a birding group he led at a local avian hot spot, Mount Auburn Cemetery. Mary's story actually began as a tale about fish. When Mary had moved to a new house, she'd transported not only her furniture and her dogs, but her fish pond and its resident koi and goldfish. Koi, as I had to ask, are big fancy Japanese carp. Anyway, after installing the pond and its inhabitants, Mary found one of her koi dead at the water's edge. The cause of death was obvious: a wound in the big fish's head. Equally obvious was the murder weapon: the canine tooth of an

Alaskan malamute. Mary blamed her dogs, especially Miss Pooh, who had a fishy look in her eye, so to speak. Meanwhile, Mary was vaguely aware of occasionally hearing a loud whoosh in her new yard, a noise she dismissed because she was paying attention to the continuing disappearance of the koi and goldfish from her pond. Miss Pooh and Mr. Wookie remained the obvious culprits until one day when Mary returned home to find that yet another koi had vanished while the dogs had been in their kennels and nowhere near the pond. The malamutes having been exonerated, the fish murders remained a mystery until Mary, Miss Pooh, and Mr. Wookie not only heard the startling whoosh, but saw its source: A great blue heron was rising from the pond with a koi impaled on its beak. "It had been there all along," Mary said. "I just didn't know. I blamed my innocent dogs."

When we'd finished eating, my guests pitched in to load the dishwasher and clean up. Mr. Wookie was brought out to make friends, snack on steak, and receive congratulatory toasts, and then Rowdy and Kimi had their turn. On my own, I'd have been hard pressed to provide beer and hot dogs for this gathering. I loved being able to offer choice steak and good wine. In my contacts with Guarini and his men, I'd seen ample evidence of Guarini's wealth and no sign of anyone else's. Joey Cortiniglia's widow, Carla, hadn't had her dream of a flower shop fulfilled until after her husband's death. The bodyguards, the horrible twins, Al Favuzza, and Zap the Driver wore hideous gold jewelry, but their heavy rings and such were the only indication I'd seen of affluence.

But maybe crime did pay after all. Now that I was tasting corruption for myself, I found it mouth-watering.

Guilt held off its attack until the next morning; it waited until Mary and Mr. Wookie drove away. Then it pounced. I felt horrible. Evidence of my contamination was everywhere: in the packets of leftover steak in the refrigerator, in the empty wine bottles neatly aligned on the kitchen counter, in the unopened bottles still in the box, and most of all in the ribbons that Harry Howland had presented to Leah. Leah and I are first cousins—our mothers were sisters—but our family resemblance is limited to our love of dogs; we don't look alike. Rowdy and Kimi, too, are cousins. Their radically different facial markings mean that at first glance, they're anything but ringers. Harry Howland had been pressured to put up my dog: Rowdy. Howland had resisted, or so he'd told me; he'd certainly given Best of Breed to the dog he preferred, Mr. Wookie. But Kimi was also mine, and she'd won the points and gone Best of Opposite. Sipping my third cup of coffee, I sat at the kitchen table and watched Kimi, who was in a sphinx pose on the floor watching me. Had she deserved the ribbons? Yes. Ah, but was that why she'd won them? Exactly how had Guarini's thugs tried to influence the judge? I'd seen Favuzza speak to Harry. Had Favuzza given Howland Rowdy's number, the number on my armband? That number alone? Or the number on Leah's armband, too? What had the damned vampire said? Was that the Mob's first contact with the judge? Or a follow-up? I could hardly phone Howland to ask, and I was equally reluctant to raise the matter with Guar-

ini. As to Favuzza, I didn't have his phone number, didn't
even know where he lived, and didn't want to talk to
him. The corpse-shifting twins would know, as would
Zap the Driver. Zap seemed the most likely of the four
to give me the details without necessarily reporting back
to Guarini. And I'd see Zap the next time he delivered
Frey to me. Maybe I'd have the guts to interrogate him.
Maybe I wouldn't.

In the meantime, I could make a token effort to de-
contaminate my house. I couldn't return the steak we'd
eaten or the wine we'd drunk, and it wouldn't exactly be
a noble deed to send the leftovers to Guarini with a self-
righteous little letter ("I cannot accept your gifts, but I've
already eaten and drunk half, so here's the rest!") Still, I
could rid myself of what remained. My two big dogs, of
course, offered a convenient means to dispose of the meat.
In fact, I put them in my bedroom before dumping the
leftover steak into a plastic bag and taking it out to the
trash. The unopened bottles of wine went to the cellar,
where they'd sit until I donated them as auction items at
the annual Camp N Pack weekend of the Alaskan Malamute Rescue of New England (Visit us on the web!
www.amrone.org). I rinsed out the empty bottles and dis-
posed of them outdoors in the recycling bin under the
back steps. As penance, I then E-mailed four people
who'd applied to adopt dogs from Alaskan Malamute Rescue and were impossible candidates. It's fun to reply to
promising prospects. I picked the four least promising
applicants, people with scads of cats, rabbits, and tod-

dlers, no experience with big dogs, no kennels, and no fenced yards.

Then I cut Tracker's nails, got scratched, vacuumed, took a shower using antibacterial soap, and finally took Rowdy on leash to the smooth surface of my driveway to engage in my personal form of prayer: the merging of canine and human souls that occurs in the pursuit of flawless heeling. Heeling is alpha and omega; it's where dog training begins and ends. Good heeling does not *require* concentration; it *is* concentration. You and your dog are so lost in each other that your spiritual oneness becomes a miraculous unity of motion: You move as one.

The prayerful nature of dog obedience training is not always immediately apparent to those of conventional religious persuasions. Upon spotting a dog such as Rowdy, for example, and a person such as myself, the luckless individual who dwells in dogless ignorance and sees but through a glass, darkly, is all too likely to blurt out, "For God's sake, that woman must be crazy! She's spitting at her dog!" Cheddar cheese, in case you wondered.

To the credit of the Federal Bureau of Investigation, let me hasten to add that its agents, Victor Deitz and John Mazolla, may have sensed the spiritual nature of Rowdy's and my endeavor. Or so I like to imagine. This was, after all, Sunday morning. What I know is that the blurt-free, indeed speechless, men stood in my driveway with eyes so wide and mouths so open that I was tempted to ask whether they wanted some cheddar, too.

Our worship service having been interrupted, Rowdy and I turned our attention to the two men, who seemed to be in their mid-thirties and were short-haired, clean cut, and thus identifiable as probable non-Cantabrigians. Mormons? The Church of Jesus Christ of Latter-day Saints has a big facility on Brattle Street and sends lots of young Mormons here from Utah to try to convert the rest of us. I sometimes wonder what horrible crimes these innocent-looking missionaries have committed back home to get stuck serving out their long sentences in Harvard Square. Baptist fundamentalists would have an easier time making converts in Beirut than the Mormons probably do in this multicultural hotbed of caffeine-addicted feminist intellectuals. Not that religion is dead here. On the contrary, Cambridge is filled with people who've been Born Again: They've accepted John Harvard as their personal savior.

Or maybe the two men weren't Mormons after all. They just stood there. The Mormons were always friendly and polite.

"Are you lost?" I asked, meaning geographically, not spiritually, in other words, "Hey, this is 02138, the notorious Dip Zip, and no one as conventional as the two of you could possibly have come here on purpose."

That's when Victor Deitz, as he proved to be, asked whether I was Holly Winter. Having said that I was, I naturally expected him to tell me that his dog refused to come when called or was afflicted with submissive urination, so just as naturally I was surprised when he said, "Victor Deitz," and pointing to his companion, "John Mazolla. FBI."

Deitz was a short, hard-muscled, Nordic-looking man

with pale hazel-blue eyes and white-blond hair clipped to a uniform quarter of an inch all over his skull. Mazolla was a few inches taller than Deitz. His coloring was only slightly darker than Deitz's. His eyes were blue, his hair light brown and neatly trimmed rather than almost shaved off. Still, the two agents shared a bodily resemblance, as if they worked out in the same gym, performing the same number of reps with the same weights using the same equipment. In particular, both Deitz and Mazolla had overdeveloped, hence oversized, necks, on top of which sat what appeared by comparison to be shrunken heads. Deitz and Mazolla resembled Guarini's men in only one respect: Like the Mafia, they wore those bowling-league-style jackets.

With Rowdy's leash in my left hand, I extended my right to Deitz and said, "How do you do?" Why Deitz? A lifetime with dogs has given me an almost uncanny and definitely canine ability to recognize authority. Mine is merely a derivative gift. Rowdy, possessed of the real thing, ignored Mazolla, looked at Deitz, and returned his eyes to me. He showed no inclination to fall at Deitz's feet as he'd done at Enzio Guarini's.

"You've been keeping some strange company lately," Deitz said.

I don't like personal remarks from strangers, and from the second I met him, I didn't like this particular stranger at all. More significantly, neither did Rowdy, who showed not a trace of his usual friendliness. He didn't issue a *woo-woo* or wag his tail, and his warm brown eyes had a cold glint. When a dog who loves everyone decides to dislike someone, trust the dog.

I said, "Aren't you supposed to say what a nice day it is? Admire my dog? You're supposed to start by building a positive alliance with me. That's what I learned in journalism classes. When you're going to interview people, you start by putting them at ease, creating a cozy atmosphere."

"Miss Winter, we're not journalists. We're here about the company you've started keeping."

"The company I keep is largely canine. To the best of my knowledge, Rowdy and Kimi haven't committed a federal offense lately."

"Enzio Guarini. Alphonse Favuzza. Edward Zappardino. Thomas and Timothy Bellano."

"Edward. So that's his first name. I'm surprised. Somehow, he just doesn't look like an Edward, does he?" To Mazolla, I said, "Does your friend have something against Italians?"

It was Deitz who replied. "Miss Winter, you've got yourself caught up in something you don't understand."

"Dog training? You're wrong. I've been doing it all my life. I understand it pretty well. I just make it *look* easy."

"We've noticed that you enjoy doing favors for people. We have a few you can do for us. You're in a position to install a small number of listening devices in interesting places," Deitz said.

For a big, rough dog, Rowdy can move with remarkable grace. Now, he glided in front of me and came to a calm halt to create a sort of woofy battlement.

"I'm a dog trainer. As you can see." I pointed to Rowdy. "Enzio Guarini has a dog. A very nice dog, as it happens, a dog that does not require the investigative services of the local animal control authorities, never mind the services of the FBI. What I'm in a position to do is train the dog. That's the only position I'm in."

"We could use your help," Deitz said.

"Sorry, but there's nothing I can do."

Deitz's eyes landed on my recycling bin. "Those your wine bottles?"

"You're an ATF agent, too?"

"I've got some advice for you," Deitz said. "You don't have to do us any favors. Okay. That's your choice. But don't take any favors either. Train his dog. Leave it at that."

"No favors," I said, half to myself. "None at all."

CHAPTER 16

On my way to Carla's flower shop on Monday morning, I steeled myself to refuse any bouquets or potted plants she might offer in return for my introducing her barbaric Anthony to the fundamentals of canine civilization. I needn't have worried. Carla's little shop was jammed with silk greenery, plastic vines, stuffed animals, ceramic shepherdesses, American flags, brass tubs, decorative basketry, greeting cards, posters, and Mylar balloons. There was barely a flower or a living leaf to be seen. When I walked in, Carla was holding a can of air freshener that she'd evidently just emptied in its entirety in the small, enclosed space.

"I always love the smell of a flower shop." She greeted me. "Don't you? Oh, you brought a crate. That's nice. I never got around to ordering one. I been keeping Anthony in the car out back." His distant, muffled yaps were audible, but Carla screamed as loudly as if he were right here. Anthony had done a fine job of shaping her behavior. "Hey, I got to tell you, Frey's doing awesome."

I smiled. "Frey is a lovely pup. I'm very proud of him."

"Enzio's real happy with him."

Enzio? As recently as Joey's funeral, hadn't it been *Mr. Guarini?*

"I'm glad to hear that." I set the crate on the floor, and next to it, a big tote bag of dog-civilizing supplies.

"You want me go get Anthony?" Carla took a few steps toward the back of the shop. How, I can't imagine. Her patent leather pumps had five-inch heels. The shoes were black, as were her velvet Capri pants. Like the dress she'd worn at her husband's funeral, her frilly white blouse had a plunging neckline. Her earrings, bracelet, rings, and an ankle bracelet were gold, as was the glitter on her cheeks and eyelids.

"No," I said. "Let's leave Anthony there for a few minutes. Before we get started, we need to have a little talk about our goals for Anthony. And how we're going to go about training him."

"You want some coffee?" Carla asked. "I got a machine in the back. It's real. I hate that instant shit."

I accepted. The machine proved to be a fancy automatic espresso maker. To my delight, Carla rapidly produced two cups of incredibly delicious cappuccino, foamed milk and all. She served it in oversized cups, real, not paper. But I'm hard to distract. Once both of us were seated behind the counter of the shop, I said, "Goals for Anthony."

"I hate, like I really hate, having him locked up out there," Carla shrieked, "but I got a business to run, and I got to get him to shut up, or I can't even answer the phone."

"Perfect. First goal. Anthony will learn to be quiet."

"And he's got to leave the plants alone. He keeps digging stuff, I had to put it all away, and you can't hardly run a flower shop without plants, can you? And flowers? Maybe you noticed."

"Now that you mention it," I said. "But naturally you need to be able to have plants and flowers. Second goal: Anthony will not ruin the merchandise."

"And he don't do nothing I say. Like take Frey. You tell him sit, he sits. But Anthony? Well, you saw what he's like."

"Goal three: basic obedience. Except," I said, "I, uh, had the impression that you didn't particularly care about that."

"Well, Anthony is small," Carla said. "It's not like if he jumps on people, he knocks them over. And about what happened at Joey's funeral, it's not like Anthony goes to funerals all the time."

"We have a saying in dog training: If it's not a problem for *you*, it's not a problem. Anthony is your dog, and if you don't care whether he sits, why bother teaching him?"

Carla stirred her coffee and licked the foam off her spoon. At the lowest volume I'd heard her use, she said, "Enzio don't like it."

I bought time as she had. The coffee was wonderful. The froth was . . . well, frothy. As for Carla, she was young enough to be Enzio Guarini's granddaughter. "Mr. Guarini likes a well-behaved dog. That's true. Well, okay, we have our goals."

The phone rang. Carla excused herself to answer it. She listened and scribbled, then repeated the order to the caller: floral blanket to cover a casket, six vases of gladiolas, and a wreath of rosebuds. "The blanket's going to be super," she said. "You'll love it. For a friend of Mr. Guarini's, I'll do something real special." She then placed a phone call to order flowers. Hanging up, she said, "You ready for Anthony?"

I said yes. I *was* ready, too. I like a challenge. And I'd come prepared. While Carla got Anthony, I emptied my tote bag of its contents: a size small citronella anti-bark collar, a clicker, a leash, a container of thin-sliced roast beef, a packet of my homemade liver treats, and a copy of *The Irresistible Toy Dog* by Darlene Arden.

Anthony entered the shop between Carla's breasts. Despite the cozy traveling spot, he was screaming. Carla was screaming back at him.

"Put him down." I pointed to the floor in the middle of the shop.

The look in Carla's eye was fearful.

"I won't hurt him!" I hollered. Kneeling next to the little monster, I snapped on the leash, fastened the citronella collar around his neck, and stepped away. These collars are painless alternatives to bark-activated shock collars: The dog's barking makes the collar emit a harmless spray of citronella. Alas, some dogs don't mind citronella. Some actually like it. Luckily, Anthony hated it. The very first squirt startled him into silence. "Good boy!" I spoke calmly and gave him a minuscule bit of liver.

"This is a useful tool," I told Carla, "but all by itself, it won't perform miracles." After explaining how the collar worked, I got her to praise and reinforce Anthony for silence. Anthony's expression was comical, at once astounded and relieved.

"See how happy Anthony looks," I observed. "He knows he's a lucky dog to have someone who loves him enough to train him."

Having given Carla the crucial experience of being able to influence the dog's behavior, I moved swiftly to the proper use of the clicker. I had Carla click and treat ten times. By the tenth click, Anthony had the idea: He looked eagerly at her in expectation of a morsel of food.

"Both of you are doing great," I said. Moving far faster than I'd normally have done, I questioned Carla about Anthony, learned that he'd supposedly been taught to sit, and coached her through clicking and treating him for doing it. In the purist version of clicker training, I'd have waited for him to sit on his own, I'd have clicked and treated each time, and I wouldn't have spoken the word *sit* for a long time. I'm not a purist. But I got results. Then we stopped. "Always end a session on a note of success," I said.

Carla removed the citronella collar and returned Anthony to her car. Over second cups of cappuccino, we went over some basics of dog training: "No free lunch," I said. "If he's barking, he doesn't get anything he wants. Don't feed him, don't touch him, don't speak to him, and do *not* pick him up. Anthony has to *earn* everything." Then I gave her the book about toy dogs and instructed her about introducing Anthony to the crate. She was to leave the crate door open and encourage Anthony to explore the interior by putting toys and little treats inside. "Remember to keep the training session short," I said. "Short and happy."

"This is so nice of you!" Carla screamed.

My eyes drifted to the tiny citronella collar, which lay on the counter. Truly, there's a market for a human version. Still, I left the shop with a sense of satisfaction. Luckily, Anthony had responded to the collar, and so far, he hadn't figured out the trick of rapidly yap-yap-yapping to empty the collar of its citronella supply, thus rendering it useless. Carla had gained a sense of control over Anthony. She was highly motivated: She wanted the shop to succeed, and, surprisingly, she had what struck me as a romantic interest in pleasing Enzio Guarini. Even the shop had benefitted: Citronella smelled better than floral air freshener.

Oh, one last thing. The flowers Carla had ordered arrived just before I left. When she insisted on giving me a spray of delphiniums, my resolve weakened. I love delphiniums. And I really had done her a favor.

Damn it all.

CHAPTER 17

It took me a long time to drive from Carla's non-floral flower shop in Munford to my house in Cambridge because as usual my car staged a malamute-worthy display of disobedience. When I halted at a red light in Arlington, it stalled and then the engine flooded. As always happened on clear, dry days like that one, the windshield wipers went on whenever I signaled for a turn. The back-firing made pedestrians run for cover. Agents Deitz and Mazolla were probably too busy tailing real mobsters to follow a mere Mob-associate dog trainer like me, but I couldn't help wishing I'd catch sight of them: If the horrible Bronco quit completely, maybe I could dream up a tidbit of inside-Mafia information to trade for a ride home. After what felt like hours of annoyance and embarrassment, I eventually pulled into my driveway, got out, slammed the door, and kicked the nearly treadless front tire.

" 'Something there is that doesn't love a—' " proclaimed a quintessentially Cantabrigian voice. Robert Frost. He had lived only a few blocks from my house. Not that Frost was now speaking from the grave. The words were his, but the speaker was the female, although somewhat androgynous, owner of Kimi's attacker, the dust mop with teeth.

Finishing the quote, I said, "A wall would be a more effective means of transportation than this so-called car."

"She being *not* brand-new," the woman said. The allusion was to another Cambridge poet, e. e. cummings. In spite of the mild spring weather, the dust mop's owner wore a British-looking tweed jacket and skirt. On her feet were polar fleece socks and Birkenstock sandals. This time, the dust mop was not on the retractable leash that had given her the freedom to attack Kimi, but on a short leash.

"You will observe," said the woman, "that Elizabeth Cady's Flexi privileges have been revoked. She proffers her profuse apologies."

"Her apologies are accepted," I said.

"Ta-ta! Off we go, E. C.!" With that, she led Elizabeth Cady away.

I gave the Bronco another kick, went into the house, hugged the dogs, sat down at the kitchen table, pounded my fist on it, and burst into tears. Then I washed my face, made coffee, and called Leah. "My damn car is shot," I told her.

"No kidding."

"Leah, it's not fit to drive."

"There are holes in the floor. It backfires. It refuses to start. It stalls. The gauges don't work, and neither does the radio. For starters."

"Leah, no, it's worse than that. This isn't just the usual. I drove it today and barely made it back home. I know I promised to help you move Rita's old love seat tonight, but I just can't. I'm sorry, but if we try, we're probably going to get stuck in the middle of the Square with a dead car and a couch. I really don't dare to drive it."

"Anyone else would've dumped it a year ago."

"Well, I guess anyone else would've had the money to replace it."

"What are you going to do?"

"Walk. Damn it! The one good thing about this car was that I owned it. I cannot afford car payments. But I don't have much choice. I'm really sorry about the love seat, but it just won't fit in Rita's car."

"It'll fit in Steve's van. Easily."

"Leah, I don't like to—"

"I like to. I will. I'll call you back."

Leah hung up. Five minutes later, the phone rang again. Leah announced that all our problems were solved, by which she meant that that she and her roommates wouldn't have to wait to get the attractive and fairly new love seat Rita had offered her. Leah had interrupted Steve at his clinic and taken advantage of his obliging character by persuading him not only to let her use his van, but to help us move the love seat. In connection with Steve, the very word bothered me. *Love* seat. Why couldn't Rita have discarded a piece of furniture with a loveless name?

"There is no need to impose on Steve," I told Leah. "Your friends can help, and—"

"Steve doesn't mind. He volunteered. And he's bringing Sammy. My friends want to meet the puppy. Everyones's going to get to your house around seven."

Rita rapped on my door at six-thirty.

I greeted her by saying, "Leah is being high-handed and bossy about this love seat."

"She's doing me a favor. The new one is being delivered tomorrow, and if Leah wasn't going to take this one, I'd have to have it hauled off."

Rita is the sort of person who moves furniture by getting someone else to do it. She's perfectly fit. As is appropriate for a psychologist, the impediment is strictly mental. Well, it's also pedal, so to speak. Or podiatric? How can anyone who calls herself a feminist possibly wear high heels? That's what I asked Rita.

"To make sure I always have defensive weapons handy." She kicked off her suede pumps, took a seat at my kitchen table, and poured each of us a glass of merlot from the bottle she'd brought. "And now you're going to tell me that I could perfectly well learn to groom Willie myself and therefore *should*."

Willie is Rita's Scottish terrier. Theirs is a perfect match. They're stylish, high-maintenance creatures. Also, Rita spends her working hours trying to change her clients' behavior and refuses to come home and make the same effort with her dog. Willie, for his part, is almost untrainable—that's my opinion, anyway.

"No, what I'm going to tell you," I said, "is that I've finally given up on my car. Every mechanic I've taken it to in the past year has told me that I need to dump it. This morning, I realized that they've all been right. The thing has become outright dangerous."

Rita is sensitive to the difference in our incomes: She didn't ask why I hadn't replaced my car years ago.

I said, "It's a good thing I like walking. The second half of the advance on my liver book isn't here yet. Not that it'll buy me a new car. Meanwhile, here's Leah commandeering Steve and his van, and it's humiliating to have him know that I can't afford—"

Rita almost never interrupts. "Stop it! As if Steve cares what you drive. Or how much money you make."

Rita knows me so well that I don't have to bother explaining abrupt transitions. "Rita, how *could* he have married that horrible woman?"

"You've read *The Odyssey*. Remember Circe? She turned men into swine. Steve did what a million other men've done. You rejected him, and he fell under Anita's thrall."

"Sssshh! He's here."

Steve and Sammy the Baby Rowdy entered the kitchen trailed by my cousin and three other undergraduates, a woman and two men whom Leah must have chosen for their brawn. Leah is not only practical but polite. She introduced everyone to everyone else. Then, to Sammy's delight and to the grinning Steve's as well, she and her friends sat in a puppy-centered circle on the floor and

fussed over Sammy, handed him around, and let him un-
tie shoelaces and scramble from lap to lap. The young
woman was African-American with braided hair as black
as Leah's was red-gold. One of the young men was Eu-
rasian, the other almost comically Yankee looking, raw
boned, big footed, and lantern jawed. Together, the four
students and Sammy could've been posing for a photo
intended to illustrate the universality of dog love. Steve
and Rita shared my pleasure in the beauty of the scene;
all three of us smiled knowingly. For me, there was the
added joy of glimpsing Rowdy as I'd never seen him. Our
lives had intersected when he was a young adult; I'd never
known him as a puppy. Now I could.

Beauty is never more fleeting than in the case of a
puppy too young to be reliably housebroken. When
Sammy began to sniff and circle, Steve scooped him up
and took him out, and then all of us turned to the task
of moving the love seat from Rita's apartment to Steve's
van.

My house, I remind you, is at the corner of Appleton
and Concord. The driveway is on Appleton Street. It's
wide enough for two cars and easily accommodates two
more behind the first two. When I'd driven the ailing
Bronco home earlier that day, two cars had already been
there, side by side, Rita's new BMW and my third-floor
tenants' second car, a Honda sedan. I'd parked behind
Rita's car. Steve's van was now in back of the Honda.
Since moving the love seat didn't require all of us, Rita
and I decided to switch cars while Leah and her friends
went upstairs to get the love seat and while Steve

crated Sammy in his van. The point of trading parking places with Rita was that my expiring Bronco belonged in a spot where it wasn't blocking another car and where it could just sit until I got rid of it. After a couple of noisy attempts, I got it started, pulled out of the driveway, backed a little way down Appleton, and watched as Rita backed out and drove forward on Appleton to wait for me to take her place. That's when the Bronco quit. And not quietly, either. Imagine the painfully amplified roaring of diseased intestines. Steve's soon-to-be ex-wife, I might mention irrelevantly, drove a silver sports car, and not the kind that made racetrack *vrooms,* but the kind that made no sound at all. To Anita's discredit, her car had no room for dogs because she really hated them, whereas my Bronco had lots of space for big dogs and had transported them for thousands of miles. In fact, there's no doubt in my mind that Rowdy and Kimi were involuntarily responsible for its demise because every formerly moving part was now clogged with malamute undercoat. So, right in the middle of Appleton Street, the luckless vehicle died of dog hair.

By this time, the love seat was in the van. Rita's idea of moving broken cars is to call AAA, but everyone else helped to push the Bronco to the space on the street just beyond my driveway. To minimize the duration of my embarrassment, I insisted on leaving the Bronco there instead of trying to push it into the driveway. Steve, Sammy, Leah, her three friends, and the love seat departed. Rita went upstairs to her apartment. I ate dinner, puttered, checked my E-mail, took the dogs for a short walk, and went to bed early. Rowdy and Kimi slept on the bed. At three o'clock in the morning, both dogs were still dozing on the comforter. Almost nothing ever bothered them. Thunder didn't scare them, and they were used to the Bronco's habitual rumbling and backfiring. Regrettably, I am only half malamute. At three A.M. a thunderous BOOM not only jolted me awake, but terrified me. When I threw on jeans, a sweatshirt, and running shoes, the dogs finally got interested. They tagged after me as I dashed to the cellar, where everything there was normal. Neither the hot water heater nor the oil burner had exploded. But as I discovered when I finally looked outdoors, something of mine *had* blown up.

My Bronco.

I had good insurance. The car was worth more dead than alive. And it was now definitely dead.

CHAPTER 18

After running to the cellar to make sure that the house wasn't on the verge of petrochemical detonation, I left the dogs indoors and sprinted outside, where I nearly collided with Kevin Dennehy. When the boom had jolted me awake, I'd experienced what I suspect is the almost universal impulse to react to unidentified blasts, roars, and smells of smoke by focusing on dangers affecting my loved ones and my own property. But asleep or awake, Kevin was all cop. Awakened by the same thunderous bang, Kevin had assumed that its source was an external threat, against which it was his duty to protect not only his mother, his house, and himself, but all the rest of us, too, including, if need be, the City of Cambridge, the Commonwealth of Massachusetts, and the entire United States of America. In brief, by the time I'd finished investigating my cellar, Kevin had already gone outdoors, found the smoldering wreck of my car, and summoned what he casually called "backup."

The minute I opened the back door, the stench hit me, and my own outside lights and the streetlights let me catch a glimpse of smoke coming from my car. Kevin refused to let me near it. I protested.

"You could've been in it," he said.

"In the middle of the night? Kevin, really. It's *my* car. I want to see what happened to it."

"It blew up."

"Kevin, I can smell what happened. I want to *see* it. Where was it?"

"On the street. And the first thing I want to know—"

"I know where I parked my car. Where in the car was the explosion?"

"Where?"

"What part of it?"

"The *car* part of it. The *vehicle*."

The wail of a fire truck drowned me out. It was the first of three. Kevin had also summoned many of his brothers in blue and, for no reason at all, an ambulance and, ridiculously, I thought at first, a truck that appeared to be hauling a cement mixer. I soon abandoned the fantasy that the spontaneous combustion of dog hair had delivered the coup de grâce to my car. Malamute undercoat had killed a succession of my vacuum cleaners. When my stove had broken, the repairman had removed its top to reveal an inch-thick layer of fluff. But dog hair, even powerful malamute hair, was innocent of this destruction. As the reality hit me, I was frightened. Learning that the apparent cement mixer belonged to the bomb squad, I was glad to have the contraption there. I also felt grateful that Kevin had the clout to muster a massive amount of official help. An ordinary citizen might've screamed at the 911 operator to send every cop, firefighter, and EMT in the city; Kevin actually succeeded in jamming our narrow street with an amazing number of emergency vehicles and a slew of wonderfully calm, capable emergency professionals.

Residents were there, too. Kevin ordered the immediate evacuation of my house, his own, and the two across the street. I obeyed the order and, as probably goes without saying, imposed it on my animals. A uniformed officer carrying Tracker's carrier shepherded the dogs and me out my back door and down the driveway. As the officer tried to hustle Rowdy, Kimi, and me down Appleton Street, we passed close enough to the Bronco's earthly remains for me to get a good look. Ignorant though I was about all things automotive, I did know that the Bronco's engine was in the front. My view of the car was pretty good, albeit somewhat weird and melodramatic. In addition to the ambient brightness in any city, illumination now came from the windows of the houses along Appleton Street, and from the headlights and the flashing red lights of the emergency vehicles. Oddly enough, although Rowdy and Kimi often answer the call of sirens with malamute howls, the dogs remained silent in the midst of the cacophony, perhaps because they could see that its sources, although big and noisy, were non-canine and, indeed, inanimate.

I've drifted from the point, which isn't the intelligence and unflappability of my wonderful dogs, but the post-explosion condition of my horrible car. As I was starting to say, even my scant knowledge of automobiles led me to expect that if a Bronco's engine combusted, the subsequent damage would be worse toward the front of the car. In fact, my Bronco's hood was intact, but the rear and side windows were shattered, and jagged metal fragments framed a new and large hole in the rusty body behind the doors. Kevin's reaction now made sense. The engine hadn't exploded. Yet.

I quit dawdling and gaping, and instead of ignoring the hurry-up shouts of the cop who had Tracker's crate, I screamed back at him over the din, and with Rowdy and Kimi leading the way, ran down Appleton Street toward Huron Avenue. Fear drove me, fear inspired less by the sight of my ruined car than by hideous visions of the possibilities. My car hadn't just exploded; it had been blown up; someone had rigged it to detonate. Deitz? Alternatively, the vaporization of my Bronco could have been a Mob favor. If so, it could easily have become no favor at all. Had the bomb been on a timer? What if there'd been a miscalculation and the explosion had occurred during the previous evening? What if I'd declared the car fit for use and Leah and her friends had loaded the love seat into it instead of into Steve's van? What if Steve and little Sammy had been standing on the sidewalk next to the car when it exploded?

Reaching the crowd at the far end of the block, I sank to my knees and wrapped my arms around my dogs. I could feel the strong beat of Rowdy's heart. The initial boom, the excitement, the lights, the sirens, and the dash down the street simply *must* have elevated his heart rate. But what I felt through my fingertips was a steady, slow rhythm. Out of curiosity, I felt for Kimi's heart. Its rate matched Rowdy's. I let myself sink between the dogs. I like to imagine that I'm half malamute: rugged and brave. Unfortunately, I belong to a lesser breed. Proof: I was frightened and frantic. No matter how long I live with this breed of breeds, I'll never become even half malamute. I'm incredibly uncool. The Alaskan malamute is ultimately Arctic, too cool for words.

"You know what, guys?" I said. "If I'd set out to destroy that car and nothing else, I couldn't have done a better job than this. And that, I think, is exactly what someone did."

CHAPTER 19

Translated into English, the typical dog message takes the form of a single present-tense first-person sentence: I like that, I hate that, I feel sick, I feel stressed, I'm thirsty, I'm rivalrous, I need to go out. As a dog professional, I allow myself the freedom of rich interpretation. In particular, I'm willing to shift the canine present to the future. The change of tense inevitably entails— no pun intended—muddying the plainspoken all-about-me here-and-now of canine sentences with messy human attributions of conditionality and probability. If I reach toward a dog's neck and he bares his teeth at me, what he means is *I'm scared*. According to my rich interpretation, he also means, *Grab my collar, and I'll nail you*. To avoid getting bitten, I'll act on my interpretation, but it will remain *mine*; all the dog will actually have told me is that he's desperately frightened.

As a dog trainer, I'd never claimed expertise in decoding human messages. Now, as dog trainer to the Mob, I had no clear idea how to interpret the cryptic message delivered by whoever had blown up my car. According to Kevin, the culprit was no amateur. Like everyone else in dogs, I know hundreds of professional dog trainers, dog writers, dog photographers, dog artists, pet-food company representatives, veterinarians, vet techs, groomers, and handlers. By comparison, my acquaintanceship in the world of automobile exploders was pitifully small.

"Not that I want to expand it," I told Tracker, who wasn't listening. It was Tuesday morning. I felt better than you might expect, shaken but also relieved: scared about what might happen next, but glad that my horrible car would never again endanger anyone. The dogs felt dandy. The emotional casualty was Tracker, who was in the kitchen huddled over the saucer of canned cat food I'd offered her in the hope of soothing her frayed nerves. The dogs were in the yard so that Tracker could have the run of the house. Instead of displaying a healthy curiosity about her surroundings, she alternately chomped at her Fancy Feast and glanced fearfully left and right.

I kept talking, not because poor Tracker actually liked my voice, but because I couldn't believe that any creature was impervious to my soothing tones. I said, "As to decoding the message, the problem, you see, is that I can't tell what effect the explosion was supposed to have on me. Most people are about as delighted to have their cars blown up as they are to be shot at. I, as you know, am an exception. As I did not inform the insurance company when I called this morning, I am immensely happy to be rid of that damned rattletrap. Furthermore, I'd've had to pay a dealer to take it as a trade-in, whereas now, the insurance company is going to pay me for my supposed loss."

To hold my audience, I sprinkled Tracker's food with Kitty Kaviar.

"Ah, but not everyone knows that I'm the exception. Agents Deitz and Mazolla, for example. The Boston office of the FBI, my dear Tracker, has an impure record. Shocking! The corruption there consisted primarily of recruiting the notorious Blackie Lanigan as an informant. The quarry then was Enzio Guarini. The quarry *now* is Enzio Guarini. Asking me to spy on him didn't work. Blowing up my car was, I remind you, a professional job. And FBI agents *are* professionals."

Having gulped down all the Fancy Feast and Kitty Kaviar, Tracker bolted for my study. I closed the door behind her. It would've been kinder, really, to let her enjoy the treats in solitude in that one little room. People newly sprung from prison are popularly believed to suffer from anxiety and disorientation induced by unaccustomed freedom. In the TV footage I'd seen of Enzio Guarini's arrival home after his release, he'd looked relaxed and cheerful, probably because he'd already put down a deposit on an elkhound puppy.

After letting in the dogs, I called Guarini, not to inquire about the power of puppy purchase to cure post-prison stress syndrome, but to cancel today's puppy kindergarten. Before placing the call, I'd debated about how to phrase the tidings of my Bronco's demise. The news wouldn't necessarily be news to Guarini, but I intended to present it as such. Unlike Deitz and Mazolla, Guarini knew all about my wreck of a car. So did his men. At Saturday's show, in front of Zap, Favuzza, and the monster twins, I'd complained about discovering the rusted-out hole in the floor.

Guarini was grateful to me. The steaks. The wine. The Bronco?

I settled on saying, "My car's out of commission. Permanently. It's been towed off. I'm sorry to cancel, but I'm sure there's a mess out on the street from it that I'll have to clean up, and I have to figure out what I'm going to do."

Guarini was a model of paternal solicitude. "Rowdy and Kimi, they're safe. You're safe. That's what matters." As I've said, Guarini was a real dog person. His concern for my dogs and me, in that order, may have explained his failure to inquire about the cause of the car's demise. He went on to update me on Frey and to thank me for helping Carla with the horrible little Anthony. *Horrible* is my word, not Guarini's. Guarini had nothing bad to say about Anthony, and on the subject of Carla, he was practically effusive. "Carla's a nice girl," he said. He repeated the phrase. "A nice girl. A beautiful girl. Too young to be a widow. It's a shame."

I was tempted to utter a platitude about the heartbreak of heart attacks, thereby demonstrating my acceptance of the boss's declaration that Joey's murder hadn't happened. But Guarini wouldn't want mere compliance; he'd want obedience. Consequently, I said nothing about Joey's death. In that respect, this conversation was typical of every interchange I ever had with Enzio Guarini: Except when we talked about dogs, everything important always went unsaid. In that sense, my relationship with the Dogfather bore an unsettling resemblance to my relationship with Steve Delaney. And just what would Rita have to say about that observation?

"Anthony is a challenge." I said. "Retraining him is going to be slow. I hope Carla understands that."

"Carla's got a big heart," he said. "She's just got to learn to say no."

"That's hard with a cute little dog."

It's hard with a notorious crime boss, too. As I didn't add, but wanted to: "No, don't send food! No, don't send wine! And don't you ever again try to influence an AKC judge!"

After hanging up, I gathered the supplies I thought I'd need to clean up the area where the Bronco had been parked. As I did so, I wondered, as I'd done before, whether Guarini's men had carried out his orders in trying to influence Harry Howland or whether they'd acted on their own. Many years earlier, Guarini had finished two elkhounds. He hadn't handled the dogs himself, but he'd owned them, and he understood the rules of the dog show game. The clumsiness—the plain stupidity—of the effort to sway the judge pointed toward Guarini's underlings; one thing no one ever called Guarini was *stupid*. At a guess, Guarini had told his thugs to help me out at the show, and they'd interpreted the order in a way Guarini hadn't intended. Had Guarini ordered his henchmen to "help" me with my car, too? I liked the possibility, mainly because it let me read the explosion as a message of thanks rather than as a threat of worse to come.

"But we don't know, do we?" I said to the dogs. "All we know is that I've got a mess to clean up."

The firefighters had sprayed my car with chemicals. I intended to hose down the street and sidewalk and to sweep up any auto glass that might remain. To my amazement, there was nothing to clean up. As I stood gaping at the tidy, clean, and wet space on Appleton where my car had been, Mrs. Dennehy backed out of her driveway, lowered her window, and called out, "My Kevin sent them." Before I had the chance to tell Kevin's mother to thank him, she drove off. When Mrs. Dennehy speaks of *they* and *them* in reference to Kevin, she means city employees, whom she views as her son's employees. I've never had any reason to think that Mrs. Dennehy over-estimates Kevin's power in this city. Anyway, as I was standing there with a dopey, appreciative smile on my face, along came the ever-so-Cantabrigian owner of Kimi's attacking dust mop. Today, the dog wasn't with her, and she was riding a bicycle. I'd seen her on it a few times before. It was an old black three-speed women's bike with a basket in front that at the moment held three hardcover books in plastic jackets. The Observatory Hill branch of the Cambridge Public Library was right around the corner on Concord Avenue, directly across from the front door of my house. The books weren't the volumes of poetry I'd have expected, but they weren't a surprise either: novels by Mameve Medwed, Stephen McCauley, and Elinor Lipman, all of whom are, I think, literary descendants of Jane Austen by way of Barbara Pym, and somehow deeply Cambridge even though Lipman neither lives in Cambridge nor sets her novels here.

Pointing to the books, I smiled and said, "I loved every one of those."

To my disappointment, the woman just nodded and kept on pedaling instead of stopping to play the great Cambridge game of exchanging book recommendations and information about which authors were signing when at nearby bookstores. Even so, the little encounter, combined with the unexpected absence of broken glass and chemical foam, left me happy with everything about Cambridge, everything being town and gown. In this instance, Gown, in the person of the dust mop woman, hadn't supplied me with the title of a book or the name of an author I just *had* to read, but Town, in the person of Kevin Dennehy, had more than compensated for Gown's lapse by sparing me a nasty clean-up. And if I wanted recommendations for novels, I could stop any stranger on the street. In the vicinity of Harvard Square, *Read any good books lately?* is recognized as the urgent question it is and always receives the thoughtful, enthusiastic answer it deserves.

I did not, however, go back inside to cozy up with a good book. Rather, I phoned Steve's clinic to cancel Sammy's visit, and accepted condolences on the loss of my car from the vet tech who took the message. After hearing that I needed groceries, she offered me the use of Steve's van. I said no thanks. Next, I called Leah. My emotions were bouncing back and forth between relief and fear. Fear was now on the rise. In spite of the professional skill that had gone into blowing up the Bronco, Leah might have been maimed or killed. Even before last night, my Mob connections had crept disquietingly close to my cousin. At the show, the creepy, vampirish Favuzza had ogled Leah. The memory made me queasy.

I caught Leah as she was about to leave for a class. "I'll be quick," I said. "I just wanted you to know that my car's dead. It, uh, blew up, more or less. In the middle of the night."

"Are you okay?"

"Yes. It's just that I can't stand to think how close everyone was to it last night. You, your friends, Rita, Steve, Sammy. I feel unnerved. I just wanted to touch base with you. That's all."

"Well, I'm fine. I wasn't in your car."

"Also, Leah, I wanted to mention . . . those, uh, people who were at the show . . ."

"The ones you were so unfair about?"

"I was not! Leah, you haven't heard from . . . ?"

"No, but if I do, I won't be a snob like you."

"Leah! That is—"

"Holly, the first time I met that man—what's his name? You know. The one with the widow's peak. When I met him was outside the Museum of Fine Arts, you know what he really wanted?"

"You," I said.

"He wanted to know whether there were real mummies in the museum, and he wanted to know what you had to do to get in. I told you before. He did not understand that he could just walk in. Holly, it's a terrible thing that anyone should feel so marginalized, so excluded from society! Can you imagine that? And here you are—! Incredible! Not everyone has had your advantages, you know."

There ended the conversation. Leah went off to her class. The subject, it so happened, was sociology.

CHAPTER 20

Edward Zappardino possessed multiple disadvantages. For once I'm not referring to dogs. It's true, however, that he'd never owned one. Too bad, because a dog wouldn't have minded his lack of such physical and mental attributes as a handsome face, a fine physique, high intelligence, and a charming personality. Zap's dog, had he ever been blessed with one, would have seen him as altogether admirable in body and mind. As proof that my psyche has not gone entirely to the dogs, let me say that unlike the proud canine Zap might have owned, I was embarrassed to be seen with him, especially in so public a place as Loaves and Fishes.

You will recall that Loaves and Fishes was the natural foods supermarket in back of which Joey Cortiniglia had been murdered. Zap and I were not, however, on a sentimental revisit to the scene of the crime. I was doing my grocery shopping. Zap had driven me because Enzio Guarini, taking pity on my carless state, had insisted on sending me his limo and, with it, his driver. When Zap had pulled into the supermarket parking lot, I'd assumed that he'd wait behind the wheel while I shopped. Unfortunately, he'd said, "You mind if I come along?"

I'd lied in saying, "Not at all."

By way of thanks, he'd said, "It gets boring as shit being stuck in the car all the time."

As I've mentioned in passing, Loaves and Fishes is a temple devoted to the worship of wholesome holistic organic purity in all things: food, vitamin supplements, cosmetics, detergents, paper products, and esoteric personal-care devices, such as peculiarly shaped toothbrushes and spiked wooden implements designed to clean and massage your feet while moving you toward Oneness with the Infinite. As Zap remarked while we strolled amidst the fruits and vegetables, "This shit's friggin' weird."

Actually, he was referring to avocados. He'd never seen them before and had no idea what they were.

Sounding ludicrously like Julia Child, I said, "They're perfectly delicious." I felt entitled to sound at least a little bit like Julia because once my new book was released, I'd be a cookbook author, too, although granted, *101 Ways to Cook Liver* wasn't exactly *Mastering the Art of French Cooking*. For a start, the recipes weren't French. There were other trivial differences as well. Still, in researching the book, I'd finally learned to cook and on occasion did so for myself as well as for the dogs. Liver was no longer in my repertoire. Julia was probably tired of coq au vin, too.

Zap didn't recognize fresh ginger, either. I managed to silence him when he started to say what it looked like. It was easy to understand why Al Favuzza was always telling Zap to shut up. I did, however, see Leah's point about marginalization and disenfranchisement. When I put a bunch of fresh basil in my cart, Zap asked me what it was. This from a guy named Zappardino!

"Basil," I said. "It's Italian. No one in your family cooks Italian?"

"I don't eat home much. I sleep there, but I'm out a lot."

"You live with your parents?"

"My mother. My sister and her husband and their kids are upstairs." As if he needed to apologize for living at home, he said, "Saves on rent." Instead of letting the explanation stand, he added, "But don't get me wrong. I got prospects. It might look to you like I'm an errand boy, but, hey, you gotta start somewhere, right? What are you buying that stuff for?" Zap pointed at the mesclun mix I was putting in a plastic bag.

"For salad," I said.

"You know, that stuff, those little leaves, all that is, is just what they're trying to get rid of. You ought to get yourself a head of lettuce and not let these people take advantage of you."

"I *like* this stuff. It might not look like much to you, but let's say that it's got prospects, okay?"

My pleasantry didn't go over big with Zap. His scrawny body stiffened, and he glared at me.

"Hey, I was just joking," I said. "This is fancy gourmet lettuce, and I'm sure that right now you're serving a sort of apprenticeship. Before long you'll be on your way up."

We were now at the meat counter, appropriately so, I thought, since the butchered steaks, roasts, and pieces of stew meat probably provided a vivid foreshadowing of Zap's vocational future.

"Take Joey," he said.

"What?"

"Joey started out like me, you know, low level. And look where he ended up."

Unable to contain myself, I said, "Underground?"

"Before that."

"Before that, Joey—" I gestured toward the rear of the store, beyond which lay the parking lot where Joey Cortiniglia had been killed.

"Forget about that."

Impulsively, I said, "Mr. Guarini was not happy about it." I came close to adding that Guarini had ordered his men to get him the name of Joey's killer. Zap would know whether Guarini now had the name he'd sought. I stopped myself. For all I knew, the explosion that had destroyed my car was a reminder to keep my mouth shut about Joey's death. For all I knew, my message, if it was one, had come from the same gangster who'd shot Joey.

Having lost my taste for meat, I moved to the seafood department. If you've seen *The Godfather*, you'll realize that the sight of the fish counter didn't exactly rouse my appetite, mainly because the items arranged amidst the crushed ice and parsley included two whole salmon, which is to say, two whole fish, in other words, fishes, as in what Luca Brasi sleeps with.

"Bean curd," I said. Bean curd is flavorless and slimy. Ordinarily, I hated it. Now, I felt a sudden, sharp craving for it. To the best of my knowledge, tofu had never carried a Sicilian message.

CHAPTER 21

Zap, of course, limoed me home from Loaves and Fishes. Fishes! The damned Sicilian messages were everywhere. If we'd passed an establishment called the Horse's Head, I'd've died of fright. We didn't. But what awaited us at my house was worse than the imaginary, if ubiquitous, intrusion of sinister symbolism. It was real. It was the FBI.

Parked in my driveway was a beige sedan so neutral and ordinary that its only distinguishing feature was its absolute blandness. Agent Deitz was standing next to it. Mazolla was with him. As Zap began to turn the limo into the driveway, I said, "Stop! Here is fine."

"In the street?"

"Yes. Right here. Don't get out. I'll get the groceries."

Zap's prospects for advancement in Guarini's organization, or for that matter, any other, were looking worse every second. Deitz and Mazolla didn't have FBI spelled out in big letters across their jackets, but an ambitious Mob apprentice should've been able to spots Feds without having them labeled as such. Or so it seemed to me. For their part, Deitz and Mazolla wouldn't have any comparable difficulty in guessing Zap's occupation; they wouldn't even need to see him. They'd already seen quite enough. Guarini's limo might as well have had Boston Mob professionally painted on both sides complete with Enzio Guarini's phone number and a suitable logo, such as a pair of cement shoes or a horse's head.

"You don't want to meet my company. *Stay in the car,*" I told Zap. That's *stay* as in "Sit. Stay." When I speak to people as if they're dogs, it's sometimes a mark of respect. But not now. "The second I get the bags out, drive off."

My five brown paper Loaves and Fishes bags were on the floor in the rear of the limo. It took me about two seconds to get myself and my groceries out. As soon as I shut the rear door, Zap obediently took off, leaving me there at the curb. Instead of graciously rushing to carry my bags, the agents stayed by their car.

"Mr. Deitz," I said. "Mr. Mazolla. How kind of you to go out of your way to help me with my groceries. I'm deeply moved. It's always so gratifying to make new friends."

"You've got a lot of friends," Deitz said.

"Be nice to people, and people will be nice to you," I said. "I learned that training dogs—the power of positive reinforcement." To give myself something to do, I shifted the bags to the sidewalk. I thought about carrying them indoors, but I didn't want Deitz and Mazolla inside my house.

"Too bad about your car," Deitz said.

"A heartfelt loss."

"Could've been worse. A lot worse."

"I'm told it was a professional job. Come to think of it, you're a professional yourself, aren't you?"

"So's your friend Guarini."

"So is Blackie Lanigan," I said.

"Is Blackie among your acquaintances, too?"

"Don't be ridiculous. Everyone in Boston knows that Blackie Lanigan's best friends were in your office. And maybe still are. A lot of people assume that's why he's never been caught. And if I had the vaguest idea where Blackie is, I'd be the first person to speak up. For one thing, he belongs in jail. For another, I could use a million dollars. But you aren't eligible for the reward, are you? Catching Blackie is supposed to be a routine part of your job."

"All in a day's work," Deitz said. "Catching bad guys. This job would be a lot easier with a little cooperation."

"If I knew where Blackie Lanigan was, I'd tell you and everyone else. Or do you mean Mr. Mazolla? Has he been having problems with cooperation lately?"

"I'm talking about Enzio Guarini."

"You know where *he* is. That's no mystery."

"All I'm asking for is a little cooperation in putting him back where he belongs."

"Repeat! I am Mr. Guarini's dog trainer. I'm happy to

tell you anything you want to know about his puppy. Name: Frey. Breed: Norwegian elkhound. Progress: excellent. Knows sit, down, stay. Lovely puppy. Recall is remarkably reliable for his age. He heels decently for me, not so well for his owner. No longer jumps on people. Owner is grateful to me. Therefore, when he heard about my car, he sent someone to take me out for groceries. So there you have the case against him: coming to the aid of a carless dog trainer. You better go grab him and charge him and lock him up before he gets away."

"We can offer you protection."

"I am a dog trainer and a dog writer. I don't see how that makes me a candidate for the Witness Protection Program."

"You ride in Guarini's limo. You frequent his house."

"I don't *frequent* it. I've gone there to *train* his *dog*."

"Bad things happen to Guarini's friends, Miss Winter. And to his employees. Take Joey Cortiniglia."

"I attended Joey Cortiniglia's funeral so there'd be a dog trainer handy in case there was a problem with his wife's *dog*. There *was* a problem. I solved it."

"Some problems aren't all that easy to solve. Your car situation, for instance."

"I'll get another one. In the meantime, I can walk. I like to walk. I walk my dogs all the time."

"So far."

"What's that supposed to mean?"

"Like I said, bad things happen. To people. To cars. What happened to that Bronco of yours could've been a whole lot worse." He paused. "Think about cooperating."

"I *am* cooperating."

"Your dogs could've been in that car."

"Leave my dogs out of this."

"Rowdy and Kimi."

"They are none of your business."

"Let's keep it that way," Deitz said.

CHAPTER 22

"That corrupt son of a bitch threatened *my* dogs," I said to Kevin Dennehy, who was impaling an artichoke heart on his fork. We were sharing a serves-six antipasto platter at a small Italian restaurant that had just opened. The proprietor was a cousin of Kevin's girlfriend, Jennifer Pasquarelli. The place was in Watertown, just over the line from Cambridge, and occupied a storefront between an Armenian bakery and an Armenian greengrocery. The restaurant was called the Bella Vista. Our table by the window gave a view of the shops across the street and some light traffic. The vista was thus not precisely *bella*, but the food was great. Once true foodies discovered the Bella Vista, it would, I predicted, be packed with happy eaters. That night, only two other tables were occupied, both at the back of the room. As Jennifer's boyfriend,

Kevin had been given the best seat in the house.

I went on. "And as you know, I do not use the word *bitch* lightly. Kevin, I know I should've asked for help before, but—"

"You wanted to keep Guarini happy."

"Which I've done, at least until today. Zap is practically simpleminded, but by now, he's got to have told Guarini about what happened when we got to my house, and Guarini is anything but simpleminded. He'll definitely have worked it out. And he won't necessarily blame me. He likes me. Among other things, he's read my column and my articles for years. He's a fan. Guarini's not the one I'm most afraid of, anyway. I know who Enzio Guarini *is*, Kevin. I get it. But he would never hurt my dogs. The one who scares me now is Deitz."

"That asshole," said Kevin. "Pardon my French."

"There's nothing to pardon. I'm glad to have my opinion confirmed. And I have to tell you that it's a relief to talk about this. Rita is easy to talk to, but in her own way she's very judgmental. And Steve, well, just when we were starting to begin to get back together, I didn't want him to know anything about any of this. I should've told *you*, but the last thing I wanted Guarini to think was that I'd . . ."

"Gone to the cops. Start at the beginning. Take your time. There's no hurry."

I ate some marinated mushrooms and a fat pepperoncini. "It started when the dogs and I got abducted in Enzio Guarini's limousine. My best guess is that Guarini just told his thugs to pick me up and give me a ride or something, but that's not how it felt at the time. Anyway, all Guarini wanted from me was help with his puppy. He really loves dogs."

"And Mama Mia and apple cannoli. Have these thugs got names?"

"Zap. I mentioned him. The driver. Zappardino, his name is. He thinks he's on his way up in the organization, but it's a miracle that he ever learned to operate a motor vehicle. No one's ever going to promote him beyond that. The other ones were Al Favuzza—he looks honest to God like Dracula—and Joey Cortiniglia."

"The late."

"I'm getting to that."

The waiter cleared away our plates and the antipasto platter, now empty. He returned with two orders of linguini with white clam sauce. The pasta was fresh, and the sauce had tons of garlic and olive oil.

"Favuzza's some kind of distant cousin of Guarini's," Kevin said. "His specialty's the dirty work."

"With these people, that's everyone's specialty."

"Not like it's his. Holly, you don't want to hear about it. Especially not while you're eating. Anyone else?"

"There are these colossal twins. Monstrous. Gargantuan. Timmy and Tommy. When we got to Guarini's house, they were there."

"Triplets."

"Twins."

"Triplets. Bellano. Timmy, Tommy, and Teddy, except that what happened to Teddy was that he spent some time under a railroad bridge near the Neponset River.

And after that, he didn't look as much like Timmy and Tommy as he did before. Hey, speaking of which, where's that picture you were going to get for me?"

The promised picture was a photo of Blackie Lanigan. Months earlier, I'd explained to Kevin that it was possible not simply to print web pages but to download images, edit them, and print them out. Choosing an example I'd thought would interest him, I'd said that I could go to the FBI web site, capture one of the pictures of Blackie Lanigan, enlarge it, and print him a copy. Kevin had asked me to do just that. What now prompted Kevin to remind me about the photo was the notorious link between Blackie Lanigan and the Neponset River, the banks of which served as graveyard for Blackie's victims. TV shows and newspaper and magazine articles of the "Where's Blackie?" genre invariably included accounts of bodies unearthed in Quincy from the shores of the Neponset River and in Dorchester at Tenean Beach. In case you're unfamiliar with Massachusetts, let me warn you that if you visit here and feel like going to the beach, Tenean—otherwise known as Tincan Beach—is conveniently close to Boston, but it's not a place where you want to encourage your dog to dig for bones or where you want to provide your children with pails and shovels so they can have fun in the sand.

"I'll do the photo for you, Kevin. Sorry. I forgot."

"Let's get to Joey C."

"Okay. Well, let's really back up. When Guarini got out of prison, there was a lot of speculation in the news that Blackie Lanigan was going to welcome the opportunity to get rid of Guarini—that Blackie'd come back to Boston. It seemed to me that the media were probably using Guarini's release as an excuse to do more "Where's Blackie?" stories. But Guarini seemed to take the idea seriously. At any rate, he was fairly paranoid about being in public. He refused to take Frey, his puppy, to classes, and he wouldn't even let me take Frey to puppy kinder-garten. But it's impossible to get a dog used to people and noise and so on without exposing him to public places. And Frey really needed that exposure. He was ner-vous about ordinary stimuli. Bicycles." I took a break to eat. "Also, the point was to have Frey listen to his owner and not just to me. Guarini understood all this. He agreed to meet me near Loaves and Fishes so he could work with Frey in back of the mall, without a lot of distractions, and in front, where there were shopping carts and people. He showed up with his two bodyguards—not the twins, the other two—and Zap, Favuzza, and Joey. So, the dog training went very well."

"Hey, so what's the problem?"

"The problem is, was, became evident when Guarini and I got back to where we'd parked the cars, and there was Joey Cortiniglia's dead body. He'd been shot in the head. That's when the horrible twins turned up. They moved Joey's body into a car. A Suburban. Someone men-tioned Blackie. And Guarini said he wanted a name. Why, I don't know. Why would he care which hit man Blackie had used? Or maybe he thought the killer wasn't Blackie at all. He didn't confide in me. But everyone did seem to assume that the real target was Guarini, that

killing Joey was a way of getting to him. Anyway, Guarini told me that none of it had happened, and he sent me
home. Next thing I knew, Joey had died of a heart attack,
and there I was at his funeral."

"Guarini maybe didn't want to take the credit himself?"

"That's what Deitz thinks. Or what he hints at. I'll get
to him. So after Joey's funeral, I thought I had things
under control. Not everything. But my involvement. I'd
train Guarini's dog, he'd be happy, and he'd disappear
from my life. Meanwhile, he was sending people to me
for help with their dogs. Joey's widow, among others.
Carla. She and Guarini have something going. She'd always wanted to be a florist, and Guarini bought her a
flower shop, and not just as a way of taking care of a
gangland war widow, either. But I did a good job with
the dog problems. I'm good at that."

"I'm sure you are."

"And when I'm *that* motivated, I'm really good. Then
on Saturday, this past Saturday, my plan went to pieces."
I fortified myself for confessing my shame by digging into
the linguine. Italian food honestly is comfort food. "You
may not think that this is any big deal, Kevin, but it is
to me." Between bites and swallows, I told him about the
show: the attempt to influence the judge and my horror
at my betrayal of sportsmanship and friendship. "I'll never
know whether Kimi won fairly or not. It makes me sick
to think that because of me, Mary and Leah had contact
with these . . . criminals. I feel as if I've infected so many
good people with this disease of mine—Harry Howland,

Mary Wood, Mr. Wookie, Leah, Kimi, Rowdy. At the show, it was absolutely clear that Favuzza intended to do me a favor—making sure my dog won. I think that it was his idea and not Guarini's, but—"

"Guarini didn't send you any presents?"

"Oh, yes he did. Kevin, I infected you, too! The steak you ate at my party on Saturday, the wine you drank, those were presents from Enzio Guarini. I should've asked him to pay me to begin with. But not me! I didn't want to touch his dirty money. I was too noble." I practically buried my face in my pasta.

"He didn't send cold cuts? That's his usual."

"He's more grateful to me than that. For training Frey. And also I'm helping Carla Cortiniglia with her dog, Anthony, and let me tell you, Anthony acts like a little monster. Or did. Guarini could never put up with a dog like that for long. I think that his agenda is that I get Carla's dog shaped up, and then the romance can proceed."

"She interested in him?"

"Very, I'd say."

"Convenient that her husband's out of the picture. Like they say, God helps those who help themselves."

"Carla? If she was in the Loaves and Fishes parking lot or anywhere near there, I didn't see her. And she'd have been hard to miss. Carla's quite flamboyant. Or convenient for Guarini? I started to tell you before. That's what Deitz seems to think. On the one hand, Guarini can obviously hire anyone to do anything, so it's possible that he arranged to have Joey killed. On the other hand, Deitz is out to get Guarini, and my guess is that as far as Joey's murder goes, what Deitz has on Guarini is just his own bias. But I don't know. What I do know is that I've had two visits from this guy Deitz and his partner, Mazolla, and Kevin, I don't trust Deitz at all. What he wanted from me, and what he stills wants, is to have me plant listening devices. The first time, I said no. Then my car blew up. And today, there was Deitz again, only this time, he was more vague about what he wanted, and he was making not-so-veiled threats. Against *my dogs*. And I will not tolerate that. Kevin, you and I are good friends. I know how law enforcement works. Legitimate law enforcement. Trying to intimidate innocent dog trainers is not part of the process. Do I strike you as a likely informant? Of course not. The likely informant against Guarini was Blackie Lanigan. Another gangster. He was an FBI informant for years. But me? Do I look to you like Blackie Lanigan?"

CHAPTER 23

"You're a lot prettier than Blackie," Kevin said, "judging from what I've seen, anyways. I'm going to be able to tell better once I've got that picture of Blackie to hang on my wall like someone promised me."

"Kevin, I'm very sorry. I'll do it right away. I'll even buy you a frame for it."

Like every other cop in Greater Boston and probably half the cops in America, Kevin had studied the photos of Blackie Lanigan until he knew Blackie's features better than I knew the faces of my own dogs. As I understood Kevin's desire for a proper portrait of the legendary mobster, it was what Sherlock Holmes would have felt if he'd had the opportunity to acquire a portrait of Professor Moriarty suitable for display on his mantlepiece as a perverse acknowledgment of respect accorded to an archenemy.

The waiter presented us with small dessert menus.

With no hesitation, I said, "Tiramisu, please."

His eyes gleaming, Kevin said, "Sounds like one of those fancy names for soy sauce."

"That's miso," I said. "It's soup. This is Italian. It's creamy. You'll like it."

Kevin was triumphant. "Gotcha! Hey, I'm Italian myself." To the waiter, he said, "Tiramisu. Double portion." When we were alone again, he said, "I been asking a few questions about Joey Cortiniglia. Nosing around."

"Because Enzio Guarini likes heart attacks."

"Fact. The man favors heart attacks. Always did. And then the dearly departed Mrs. Guarini's godson goes and becomes a cardiologist, and Mr. G. gets to like heart attacks more than ever. But like I was saying, I started asking around, and one of the things I heard was it happened in Cambridge. And another thing was, I heard a lot of talk about Blackie Lanigan. But this is the first I heard that it happened in shooting distance of my own home. And yours."

The waiter appeared with our portions of tiramisu. Probably because the restaurant was too new to have built up a clientele, the service was very fast.

"It wasn't exactly in shooting distance," I said.

"Close enough. You know, Holly, I'm going to get you out of this. And, yeah, you should've told me to begin with. But you were scared of Guarini. You and everybody else that hasn't got"—he looked down at his plate—"tiramisu for brains. But thinking you could get yourself out of it all by yourself—that was dumb. That was just plain dumb."

"I know."

"What I need you to do now is, I need you to give me a picture of what happened. At Loaves and Fishes. Everything. Who was there. Where and when. Everything. Who got there first?"

"I did. The dogs were with me. I got there early, and I parked behind Loaves and Fishes, and the dogs and I went behind the mall and across the railroad tracks, and we walked in the park. And when we got back to the car, Guarini was just getting there. Joey Cortiniglia and Al Favuzza had already arrived, I think. They were in a big silver Chevy Suburban. It was parked parallel to my Bronco, with a space in between. And that's where Zap parked Guarini's limo, in that space. Guarini's bodyguards were with him. They always are. Musclemen. Gunmen. Whatever they are. And the puppy, Frey. I was going to crate Rowdy and Kimi in my car, but Joey didn't want them locked up. He said they hadn't done anything to deserve it. So I sort of got talked into leaving them with him. I wasn't totally comfortable about it, but he was strong enough to manage them, and I was going to be nearby. And I left my car unlocked so he could put the dogs in it if he needed to." I took a break to have a few bites of dessert. "Anyway, Guarini told Joey to stay by the cars. Favuzza was supposed to walk around and keep an eye out. And Zap was supposed to drive around in the limo. And someone . . . there was some mention that Joey had money for Guarini. Maybe I heard something at this point, or maybe it was later. At any rate, what happened next was that Guarini and I worked with Frey. The bodyguards were there, too. On either side of Guarini. We went from the back parking lot past the laundromat, along the side of the building, and around the corner by the liquor store. We ended up in front of Loaves and Fishes. Then I went in there to buy some good treats for Frey."

"Alone?"

"Yes."

"How long were you in there?"

"I'm not sure. Not too long. But I did wait at the deli counter. And there was a line at the checkout. Ten minutes? Maybe five."

"Which?"

"I just don't know. What I'm sure of is that when I got back outside, Guarini was there. He was working with Frey, just the way he was supposed to. If you're asking whether he could've left and come back, I guess so, but I certainly didn't have that impression at the time."

"The bodyguards? They were still there?"

"Yes. They're always with him. So, we worked with Frey. Not for long. He's just a puppy. And then we headed back toward the cars. And I couldn't see Rowdy and Kimi. Or Joey, who was supposed to stay right there with my dogs. So as soon as I saw that my dogs weren't there, I went flying for my car. The dogs weren't in it. And then I found them. They were hitched in front, tethered to the undercarriage, one dog on one side, one dog on the other, and someone had given them bones. I don't do that. I'm always afraid that they'll bite off chunks that'll lodge in their intestines. So bones are a major treat. Anyway, that's when I saw Joey. And everyone else showed up more or less at the same time, Guarini, the guards, Favuzza, Zap and the limo. And the twins. They must've been around somewhere the whole time, but I'd never seen them before. They're the ones who did the heavy lifting. They wrapped Joey's body in plastic and moved him into the Suburban. Meanwhile, Guarini said that it—Joey's shooting—was a message to him. He wanted to know who'd sent it. Someone mentioned Blackie Lanigan. Guarini said he wanted a name. That's about it. Guarini told me that it hadn't happened. He sent me home. I went."

"Okay," said Kevin. "So we got Joey C. in back of the mall. With the dogs. Zappardino's cruising around in Guarini's car. Favuzza's on foot. And we got Tommy and Timmy Bellano. And for five or ten minutes we got Guarini and his bodyguards out of your sight. Anyone else?"

"It's a shopping mall. There were other—"

I never finished the sentence. As the final words should have been leaving my mouth, Kevin rose to his big cop feet and hurled himself across the table directly at me. As his bulk slammed into me, gunfire shattered the plate glass storefront window next to us. The next thing I knew, I was flat on the floor with a dead weight across my legs. At the back of the restaurant, people were hollering. Kevin didn't join in. Good cops don't panic. And Kevin was a good cop.

Or had been. Blood flowed from a wound in his side. Except for the flow of blood, Kevin was motionless. He was utterly silent.

CHAPTER 24

Kevin and I and the whole area around us were a mess of blood, wine, broken glass, and shattered crockery. White globs of our unfinished dessert, the tiramisu, were spattered everywhere and looked sickeningly like soft lumps of body fat or pale portions of human brain. Weirdly, I did not scream or cry or utter a single word, not even Kevin's name, and I made no effort to move my legs, which were pinned beneath Kevin's bulk. Rather, in what felt even then like a show of pseudo-competence, I managed to sit up, rip off the cotton cardigan I was wearing, and press it hard against the wound in Kevin's side. By that time, by which I mean almost no time, the wails and flashing lights of cruisers and ambulances spilled through the broken plate glass window and into the restaurant. The proprietor, Jennifer Pasquarelli's cousin, had

had the presence of mind to inform the 911 operator that the shooting victim was a Cambridge police lieutenant. The brand-new eatery, which had been almost empty of customers, was now filled with cops and EMTs.

Three hulking men lifted Kevin off my legs, which were numb. Finding me covered with blood and semi-paralyzed, two medics descended on me in search of bullet wounds. They found none. As sensation returned, my legs prickled and hurt. Kevin had collided with my left shoulder and arm, which throbbed. I felt certain that Kevin had deliberately spared my head. About six months earlier, I'd had a concussion. With Kevin and with other friends, I'd kidded around about the main piece of medical advice I'd received, which was, incredibly, to avoid another head trauma. As if on my own I'd have gone out looking for one! Kevin had remembered. With no time to think, he'd instinctively aimed himself at my shoulder and upper arm, which were padded with dog trainer's muscles, and he'd managed to avoid causing a new concussion. Stupidly, I blurted out my concussion history to the EMTs and thus ended up in an ambulance on my way to Mount Auburn Hospital. By then, I'd gleaned the information that Kevin was already at the hospital.

"He's breathing," a cop said, "but his condition's what they call 'grave.' Bad joke."

Once at the hospital, I spent a lot of time sitting on paper-covered exam tables in the bowels of the building. White-coated people poked, peered, and tapped. They asked questions about me. I asked questions about Kevin and learned only that he was in surgery and that his mother was at the hospital. My own bruised condition was all too familiar, as it would've been to anyone else who'd lived with strong, rough dogs. Over the years, I'd been knocked down, run through, and slammed into by what felt like jet-propelled brick walls. Kevin was heavier than my two dogs combined, but he'd tried to push me to safety, and he hadn't had a running start.

After the hospital staff correctly decided that I needed no treatment, I spent a few extra minutes in an exam room with a Cambridge cop named Jimmy O'Flaherty, who was a protégé of Kevin's and had a hard time questioning me about the shooting because he kept choking up. O'Flaherty had Kevin's coloring, the same fair skin, freckles, and red hair, but his build was slight, and he looked about fifteen years old.

"I'd give anything to be able to help," I said, "but I wasn't looking out the window. I was looking at Kevin. We were talking. Kevin must've seen something, though. He moved. Then I heard the shots. One second I was talking to Kevin, and the next second he knocked me to the floor, and I heard the shots. I thought he was dead."

"You hear anything then?"

"I'll tell you what I didn't hear. I didn't hear a car racing off. If it was a drive-by shooting, wouldn't you expect that?"

O'Flaherty didn't answer the question. "Did the lieutenant say anything about expecting trouble?"

"No. And when we were shown to that table by the window, he didn't seem to mind. But Kevin always expects trouble. He's a cop. He's always on high alert. He thinks everyone should be. You know that. Was he carrying a gun?"

O'Flaherty struggled to sound professional. "The lieutenant was armed. And he was the target. They can tell by how the window broke. If he hadn't've moved, he'd be dead."

"Do you pray?"

The kid looked stunned.

"Do you pray?" I repeated.

"Yes, ma'am."

"Then please do." I believe in delegating essential tasks for which I have no aptitude. Besides, the only sensible response I could expect to my own prayers for Kevin's survival would be the reminder that Kevin's life was in danger because of me. If I'd told Kevin everything about Joey Cortiniglia's killing as soon as it happened, Kevin wouldn't have had to go nosing around asking questions. If Kevin died, it would be my fault.

O'Flaherty asked whether I needed a ride home. My house is within walking distance of Mount Auburn Hospital, and if the dogs had been with me, I might have gone on foot, Deitz or no Deitz. As it was, I felt vulnerable and accepted the offer.

When the cop in the cruiser asked where I lived, I was so preoccupied with worry and guilt that instead of telling him that I lived next door to Kevin on Appleton Street, I gave my mailing address, 256 Concord Avenue, and consequently got dropped off at the front door of my house. On the porch next to the door was a basket of flowers professionally wrapped in clear plastic and obviously delivered by a florist. Sticking out of the plastic was a green stake that bore a small white envelope. Printed on it was my name. Muttering the Mob's favorite obscenity under my breath, I kicked the flowers and sent the basket sailing to a corner of the porch. It especially infuriated me to see tall spikes of blue delphiniums in the arrangement. Just as Guarini had sent red wine, which I prefer to white, he'd now sent delphiniums, my favorite flower.

Entering through the front door, I first checked on Rowdy and Kimi. Deitz's threat had made me hypervigilant about their safety during my absence. Before leaving for dinner with Kevin, I'd crated them in the guest room, padlocked the crates, locked the door to the room, and double-locked the doors to the house; Deitz had specified Rowdy and Kimi, and the crates and locks would have made it hard for him to get to them. Emerging from their crates, the dogs bounded around. Even more than usual, their vigor and beauty felt like undeserved blessings.

Assured of the dogs' safety, I found comfort in the sameness of my ordinary rooms. The horror of the shooting and my fear for Kevin's life had left me disoriented, and the too-bright, windowless hospital rooms had had a casino-like atmosphere of existing apart from time. The clock on the stove read 9:30. The message light on my answering machine was blinking. I pressed the play button.

"Holly, Steve," said the deep voice. "My mother died. I've got a flight to Minneapolis first thing in the morning.

Lady and India are all set here, but I wondered if Sammy could stay with you. Sorry to impose. If it's a problem, let me know."

His mother had just died, and he was apologizing? Her death was a total surprise. Steve's mother was in her early sixties, not all that old, and had always seemed robustly healthy. I called him immediately, extended my sympathy, learned that she'd died of a heart attack, and said that I'd be delighted to keep Sammy for as long as he wanted. During the brief conversation, I had to keep reminding myself that sudden, fatal heart attacks really did occur, hence Guarini's liking for them, I supposed.

"Do you want me to get Sammy now?" I asked. "I can probably borrow Rita's car. Or you could drop him off here. Now or in the morning. Whatever's best for you."

The invariable result of asking Steve any question at all was waiting while he thought over his answer. The one impulsive act of his life had been marrying Anita. Having learned from that disaster, he was now even more pensive and deliberate than he'd been before.

"I'm not real clear about anything right now," he finally said. "Sorry."

"Don't apologize. Your mother just died. You're entitled to let people help."

"My plane's real early." He paused. "Don't bother about Rita's car. I'll run Sammy over now if that's okay."

"I'm crazy about Sammy. Besides, I'm glad to help. I remember so well when *my* mother died. I know what it's like. I'll do anything you want."

"I feel so sad," Steve said. "Just so sad. That's all. I'll be there in fifteen minutes."

I hung up without having told Steve about Kevin. The omission was deliberate. If Steve knew that I was worried, he'd feel compelled to make other arrangements for Sammy. I didn't want him to have to go to the trouble.

In preparation for Sammy's stay with us, I dragged a puppy crate into the bedroom and then, on impulse, moved two big crates there, too. Having done so, I realized that I'd been acting on the principle that no one should have to sleep alone.

CHAPTER 25

Fifty percent of so-called dog training consists of starting with the right dog. Another 49 percent consists of not ruining what you started with. Now that Sammy was about to become a houseguest instead of a visitor, I took pains to avoid spoiling my dogs' potentially friendly attitude toward him. In this instance, the wrong dog would've been the same-sex dog, Rowdy. I crated him and then took care to protect Kimi from the sense that she was being displaced by an adorable rival. According to the Declaration of Canine Independence, all dogs are created unequal and are entitled to unequal treatment under benevolent human law. I intended to assure Kimi that she was still Miss Alpha in our little pack and that Sammy occupied a rank so far beneath the lowliest omega that the Greek alphabet was incapable of expressing how unthreatening and insignificant he was.

In preparation for his arrival, I put Kimi on leash and took her outside, in part so that she'd get to march back into the house ahead of the little guy. As we waited for Steve's van to drive up, I fed her liver treats and bounced around with her in the driveway, on the sidewalk along Appleton Street, and around the corner to Concord Avenue and the front of the house. This property is my principal investment and a good one; as the neighborhood has become gentrified, real estate values have ascended. The basket of flowers that I'd kicked into a corner of the porch was setting an untony tone. I retrieved it and was carrying it to the trash barrels under the back steps when Steve's van approached on Appleton Street and pulled into the driveway. Instead of depositing the demolished flower arrangement out of sight in one of the barrels, I dropped it next to the trash containers. Steve, I thought, shouldn't have to wait for condolences while I fussed with refuse.

When Steve got out of his van, I moved into his arms in a way I hadn't done for ages. Possibly by accident, Kimi didn't step between us. Steve rested his head on mine and breathed into my hair. He held me so tightly that I felt surrounded by his strength. He had the same clean smell I'd always loved. Men's cologne was something he'd never used. Now that his mother was dead, no one would give him any ever again. All her ill-chosen presents would stop: the hideous sweaters he donated unworn to charity, the incompetently embroidered wall hangings depicting dogs and cats suffering from what

Steve always maintained were easily diagnosable afflictions. He'd miss the unintended amusement her gifts had
provided. He might even miss her cooking: the lime gel-
atine salads with fake mayonnaise, the canned-soup cas-
seroles, and the other specialties of the house that I'd
slipped to her dog whenever I'd visited. Could the true
cause of her death have been that dreadful food?

"She was really a good mother," I said. "She loved you
a lot. She adored you." Consequently, she must have hated
everything about Steve's marriage to the rotten, if beautiful, Anita, but I didn't say so.

"She always liked you, Holly."

"I liked her, too. Steve, I am so sorry."

Unaccountably, Kimi had refrained from barging in on
the tenderest moment Steve and I had shared since he'd
married the human fiend. Even now, observing an
exchange that didn't include her, Kimi continued to sit
on the asphalt, but broke her silence by emitting one
loud, musical, and highly expressive syllable: *Whooooooooo.*
Her breath control is stupendous; she should give voice
lessons. Steve recognized this particular monosyllabic out-
pouring as a vocalization that Kimi reserved for special
people and special occasions. When he laughed in reply,
it was with Kimi and not at her.

Beautiful.

Except that Steve also turned to look in Kimi's direction and thus saw the demolished floral arrangement I'd
dropped next to the trash barrels. With regard to divine
punishment in the form of bad luck, let me say that although I'd recently been guilty of moral compromises in

my dealings with Enzio Guarini, I had always tried to be a good person—hardworking, kind to animals, and except in the lamentable cases of Mary Wood and Harry Howland, loyal to human friends. For whatever reason, Heaven did not reward me at this crucial moment by celestially burning out the flood lights mounted over the back door of my house. On the contrary, the floods lived up to their name by washing light all over the ruined flowers and all over Steve's face. When I'd kicked that basket, I hadn't merely tapped it with my foot; I'd smashed it to pieces. The basket lay on its side. Crushed blossoms and broken stems protruded from rips in the plastic wrapping. I might just as well have driven my foot into Steve's solar plexus and deposited him in the garbage. His face didn't fall; it plummeted. Then all expression left it.

"You have every reason to feel bitter," he said as calmly and slowly as usual. "I don't blame you. You know, I ordered those this morning, and with everything that's happened, I'd forgotten. It was a stupid thing to do. I should've known better."

"Steve—"

"Don't." He opened the door to the rear of the van, climbed in, and emerged with Sammy in his arms. Handing the puppy to me, he said, "Holly, don't. You had every reason. If you want, Sammy can stay with—"

"Of course not."

"I'm leaving my van here for you. There's no point in having it sit at the airport. I'll take a cab."

"I'll drive you to Logan."

He shook his head.

"Let me at least drive you home."

But he just handed me his keys and walked away.

CHAPTER 26

All that malarkey about love and warm puppies makes me want to throw up. Adult dogs give and receive love just as warmly as puppies do. The love I shared with Rowdy and Kimi was intense and profound. Right now, the last thing I needed was the emotional equivalent of a deep-muscle massage inflicted on painful bruises. Sammy tickled my injuries. He did his puppy-cute best to brush them lightly away.

By now, I'd examined and opened the florist's envelope that had accompanied the flowers. The basket had come from a Cambridge florist, not from Carla Cortiniglia's shop. The message inside the card had consisted of one word, the sender's name: Steve. A shaking chill had run through me. I'd turned on the oil burner and set the thermometer to seventy degrees. Then I'd made hot cocoa, wrapped myself in a blanket, and, after crating Rowdy and Kimi, let Sammy loose in the kitchen, where he skittered over to the running shoes I'd left by the bedroom door. He grabbed one, shook it hard, and paraded around with it dangling from his mouth. I know better than to confuse a puppy by letting him think that any shoe is a toy; shoes should be off limits. Now, instead of substituting a dog toy for the shoes, I let myself wallow in the healing here-and-now of Sammy's delight. Zen Buddhism is hot in Cambridge. It's half religion and half competitive sport. *I meditate for two hours a day* loses to *Well, I meditate for three hours a day and sometimes four.* The Buddhistically ambitious spend entire weekends at retreat centers in the Berkshires where they rack up scores of eight, ten, or twelve hours a day and return to Cambridge to lord it over the lazy Buddhists who wasted Saturday and Sunday sleeping late and mowing the lawn. If I'm ever hauled up before the Harvard Square Court of Meditation Enforcement and charged with failing to own one of those zillion-dollar meditation cushions, I'm sure to get off because I practice my own Zen. Now I no longer *was*—but was lost in Sammy's rapture with that old shoe.

Nirvana, even puppy-induced nirvana, is impermanent. Before bed, I checked the locks on all the windows, and double-locked and bolted the doors. Paradoxically, the small acts of precaution raised my fears for Rowdy and Kimi. Nonetheless, I remained in Sammy's thrall and slept deeply. In the morning, even before my first cup of coffee, I called Mrs. Dennehy. Kevin had done well in surgery and survived the night. His condition, she reported, had been upgraded from grave to serious. "I'm praying for Kevin, and I hope you are, too," she said severely.

It was the guilt-inducing tone of her voice that sent me to the worldwide web that morning. Specifically, I went to the FBI site, from which I captured three photos of Blackie Lanigan. *Capture,* as you probably know and as I'd explained to Kevin, refers to downloading images from web sites and has nothing to do with capturing criminals, except in this case, obviously. Once having captured Blackie in that limited sense, I printed all three portraits on glossy paper. Mrs. Dennehy had informed me that Kevin was in Intensive Care and not allowed visitors. When the ban was lifted, I'd have presents ready for him. *If* it was lifted? If he lived to have it . . . I didn't want to think about that.

Another intolerable thought was that by now Guarini must've heard and interpreted Zap's account of dropping me off yesterday: the men lounging by the anonymous-looking car, my panicked response. I considered the possibility of concocting a story for Guarini, but decided that it was more dangerous to lie to him than it was to tell the truth. Frey was due to arrive for a training session at any moment. What if his owner delivered the little elk-hound in person? If he did, I'd let Guarini take the initiative. If he asked about the men, I'd tell him who they were and what they'd wanted. If Guarini believed me, I might even plead for protection for my dogs.

Guarini himself didn't bring Frey to me, but the puppy's arrival broke the usual pattern. Instead of being chauffeured in the Zap-driven limousine, Frey was escorted by Favuzza as well as by Zap in the silver Suburban that had served as Joey Cortiniglia's first hearse. I'd seen the big car off and on since then and had assumed that it belonged to Guarini or to one of his enterprises and was a company car. Yes, as in "bad company." I was taking out the trash when the Suburban drove up with Zap at the wheel and Al Favuzza in the passenger seat. The exterior of the car was clean, but the dashboard was littered with fast-food wrappers, and the backseat was piled with debris. On top of a jacket I recognized as Al Favuzza's, a tabloid newspaper proclaimed that Hitler's nose had been cloned and had sprouted a moustache. In his crate in the rear, Frey was barking loudly.

Zap, who must've noticed that my eyes were on the junk in the car, said, "All this shit's Al's."

Favuzza told him to shut up. To me, Favuzza said, "I heard you had visitors."

"Unwelcome visitors," I said.

"Mr. G. says if they give you a hard time, you let him know."

"Thank you," I said. Then I got Frey, and the thugs drove off.

The training session with Frey went well. Not to brag or anything, but Guarini had reason to be grateful to me. In general, I'm a good dog trainer. With a gun to my head, I'm brilliant, and Frey was a bright, alert, hardworking little guy. When the puppy boys, Frey and Sammy, had their outside play time, I was careful not to give them the opportunity to practice aggressive behavior.

But I didn't have to intervene once. "I am very proud of both of you," I told the puppies. And meant it.

When Zap arrived to pick up Frey, the little elkhound was zonked out on a blanket in a corner of the kitchen, and Sammy was prancing around with his tail in the air, the devil in his eyes, and Rowdy's favorite fleece chewman in his mouth. He greeted Zap by depositing the toy at his feet. The welcome was pure Rowdy.

Zap, damn him, destroyed my delight by demanding, "How much you want for this one?"

Red hair runs in my family. Leah has it. The color skipped me, but I got the temper. It snapped. "Stop it! Sammy is not for sale. Rowdy and Kimi are not for sale. Mr. Wookie was not for sale. Stop trying to buy people's dogs! It's . . . it's . . ." I groped for the right word and, ridiculously, sputtered, "It's *inappropriate!*"

"This one ain't yours."

"Sammy belongs to a friend of mine, and he's Rowdy's son, and that makes him close enough to being mine. If you want a dog, go to a breeder or a shelter, but stop trying to buy dogs that already belong to other people!"

Zap remained impassive. He took Frey and left. At a guess, once outside my door, he muttered obscene retorts, but I didn't hear them and didn't care.

After checking on Kevin's condition—still serious—I devoted the afternoon to earning a living. My unpaid puppy training for Guarini had cut into my writing time, so I resisted the lure of beautiful spring weather and shut myself in my study with no company except the computer and Tracker the cat. Allowing myself only short breaks to refill my coffee cup and take Sammy out, I finished a column for *Dog's Life*. For that same esteemed publication, I also wrote a new-product review of (incredibly) dog litter. Whenever I imagine that all this dog lunacy has gone as far as it possibly can, it exceeds the limits of my imagination. Cat litter for dogs. Dear God! Not for malamutes, I should add. Not *yet*. Not that I know of, anyway.

Starting at about five-thirty, I fed all three dogs, took Sammy out briefly, puttered around, made myself a salad, ate it, and decided to take Rowdy and Kimi for a walk. By most people's standards, they hadn't been neglected lately, but Rowdy and Kimi weren't most people, and they were used to a lot of attention. Because of Deitz's threat, I felt apprehensive about taking the dogs out, but also because of Deitz, I felt apprehensive at home, too, and the dogs needed the kind of sustained exercise they didn't get from short dashes in my small yard. I reminded myself that the sun hadn't set; Deitz and Mazolla wouldn't try to grab or injure my dogs on city streets in the remains of daylight.

Little Sammy simply had to stay home; I couldn't safely manage Rowdy, Kimi, and the puppy. I expected to feel guilty about deserting him, but when I leashed the big dogs and peered into Sammy's crate in the kitchen, he was curled up asleep with his head resting on Rowdy's chewman. To avoid awakening him, I led Rowdy and Kimi out, and gently pulled the door shut.

The spring day lingered. I wore a short-sleeved T-shirt and enjoyed the sensation of mild air on my bare arms. To malamutes, ideal weather is five below with a fierce wind. In winter, Rowdy and Kimi will pause during our walks to savor the icy gusts. That night, we headed briskly down Appleton Street, crossed Huron Avenue, and continued uphill. Moving at a fast, confident pace somehow gave me confidence about the dogs' safety. When we reached the fancy part of Appleton Street, the gigantic houses with their manicured yards seemed to radiate the sense that nothing terrible could happen amidst such beauty and opulence. Glancing around, I kept telling myself that I was admiring my surroundings and not scanning for the approach of clean-cut men in innocent-looking cars. I eventually realized that I'd unconsciously headed in the direction of Mount Auburn Hospital. Kevin was allowed visits only from close family members, and no matter how human Rowdy and Kimi were in my eyes, they'd never fool the ICU staff into mistaking them for a Dennehy brother and sister. Although it felt comforting and secure to walk in Kevin's direction, I made the dogs turn around as twilight began to change to night, and I set a fast pace toward home.

When we got there, Sammy was gone.

CHAPTER 27

The door of Sammy's empty crate stood open. On the off chance that I'd failed to fasten it properly or that Sammy had somehow managed to open the door, I called to him and, with increasing urgency, searched the house. Sammy was a jaunty extrovert, not the kind of puppy who'd hole up in some hiding spot, especially once he heard my voice. He wasn't behind the headboard of my bed, a favorite place of Kimi's when she made off with greasy pizza cartons and other booty. I looked not only for the living Sammy but for his body. Puppies can stick their heads in small spaces, panic, writhe, and strangle. There was no sign of Sammy at all, not a puddle on the floor, not a puppy-destroyed object. Also missing was the toy I'd left in Sammy's crate, the fleece chewman that was a favorite of Rowdy's. In daring to take Rowdy and Kimi for a walk, I'd focused my fears on the wrong dogs in the wrong place; while Rowdy and Kimi had been out with me, Sammy had been stolen from my house.

Deitz had threatened Rowdy and Kimi, not Sammy. The person who'd had his eye on the puppy was Zap. I remembered the expressionless mask of Zap's face when I'd delivered my diatribe about his efforts to buy people's dogs. I'd imagined that once he was out of my hearing, he'd snarl and curse. Zap's reaction, I now thought, hadn't consisted of violent retorts. Zap wasn't exactly a man of words. I'd dissed him. In retaliation, he'd stolen Sammy.

Adrenaline made my heart pound and my brain zing. Five minutes on-line told me that Zappardino was, indeed, an unusual name. The web site showed one Zappardino in East Boston and one—aha!—at 57 George Street in Munford. In seconds, I had the address and a printed map of the neighborhood together with driving directions. Zap was stupid, but not stupid enough to let Guarini know he'd stolen a puppy that could easily be traced to me. On our recent shopping trip, Zap had told me that he lived with his mother. I was betting that he'd taken Sammy home to dear old avocado-less Mom.

Preparing to steal the puppy back, I dressed like a cat burglar. Cat, indeed! Absurd! Anyway, I replaced my T-shirt with a black turtleneck and added an old black denim jacket with oversized pockets. My equipment consisted of a leash, a mini flashlight, a small hammer, and the most non-Cambridge of objects, a handgun. I grew up in rural Maine, where firearms were ordinary, almost ubiquitous, household possessions, like eggbeaters and screwdrivers; the question wasn't why you'd own such a thing but why you wouldn't. My Smith & Wesson Ladysmith had been a gift from my father. I know how to use it. I store it safely. But please do not tell my neighbors about it. I'm enough of a misfit here already.

Steve's van needed no preparation. I put Rowdy and Kimi into Lady's and India's crates. Typically, despite his mother's death, Steve had left me a full tank of gas. To reach Munford, I didn't have to consult the driving directions, and although night had fallen, I had no trouble finding George Street, home of someone listed as L. Zappardino, who was, I hoped, Zap's mother. Closely spaced multifamily houses lined the narrow one-way street. Some houses had driveways, but off-street parking was limited, and cars were parked along both sides. A few residents had followed the practice of reserving the spots in front of their houses with traffic cones, trash barrels, or lawn chairs. In winter, lots of people throughout Greater Boston lay claim in this fashion to spaces they've shoveled, but you occasionally see parking turf staked out year round. The custom was popular on George Street. In front of number 57, a tattered aluminum chaise longue occupied an otherwise empty spot on the right-hand side of the street. A block ahead, also on the right-hand side, I found a space big enough for the van. I parked, shut off the engine, stowed my equipment in the capacious pockets of my jacket, carefully locked the van, and set off on foot toward what I thought must be Zap's house. When I'd gone no more than twenty or thirty feet, headlights appeared down George Street, and a big car approached.

I stopped. So did the car. The driver's door opened. A figure stepped out into the street, ran around the car, moved the chaise longue to the sidewalk, returned to the car, and parked it—directly in front of number 57. Immediately, the driver got out, went up the front walk, and ascended a short flight of stairs to a small porch with a light mounted over two doors. Resisting the urge to dash forward, I settled for long, rapid strides. In seconds, I was close enough to have a clear view of the big car and its driver. The car was the familiar silver Suburban. Plainly visible under the porch light was Zap, who turned a key in the lock of the left-hand door and vanished into the house. Sammy wasn't with him.

With no hesitation, I cut between two parked cars and ran down the street to the Suburban. Speed was all I had going for me, speed and the bit of luck that consisted of the Zappardino family's evident habit of keeping every blind and curtain in the house tightly shut. The porch light at the Zappardinos' house seemed to brighten and almost to shine right at me as I approached the Suburban, but that same light let me see that neither Al Favuzza nor anyone else occupied the passenger seat of the Suburban. I didn't waste time creeping around the big car and peering into the back. When I reached the driver's side door, I already had a grip on the hammer I'd brought and was about to raise it and smash the window when Zap's behavior registered on me: He'd been in a big hurry. I tried the car door. It was unlocked. But when I'd opened it only an inch or two, I heard what sounded like the banging of a storm door from a nearby house. Just

how nearby? Ducking down, I peered through the Suburban's windows. The Zappardinos' porch was just as it
had been; no one was there, and both front doors were
closed. But the false alarm scared me. If Zap had left the
car door unlocked, he intended to be right back. I had *no*
time.

I opened the car door and slipped in. Although Frey's
crate was visible at the back of the Suburban, Sammy was
loose in the backseat of the car. The mess I'd noticed
earlier hadn't been cleaned up, and little Sammy was
having a grand time. Even in the dim light, I could see
that Al Favuzza's jacket was ripped, and when I grabbed
the wiggling little malamute, he kept his jaws locked on
some treasure that he had no intention of leaving behind
or surrendering to me. Without bothering to search for
Rowdy's purloined chewman, I got Sammy out of the
Suburban, closed its door, clamped the puppy against me
with both arms, and bolted down George Street.

Once inside Steve's van, Sammy let his booty fall from
his mouth. I'd had the vague impression that it was a
magazine, but what dropped to the floor seemed to be
loose sheets of paper. I didn't bother to examine them,
but tossed Sammy into his crate, started the engine, and
drove off. All the way home, I kept checking the side
mirrors in fear that someone was following me. No one
was. On the contrary, someone was waiting for me at
home. That someone was Enzio Guarini.

CHAPTER 28

Enzio Guarini's Mobmobile occupied the parking spot on Appleton Street just beyond my driveway: the precise space where my Bronco had blown up. Pardon me. Had *been* blown up. Guarini's limo was intact. In the parlance of dog people, *intact* is a loaded word. I'm using it accurately. Like everything else about Guarini, the limousine had the unneutered air of possessing the full complement of male equipment. But I digress. The limo's headlights and taillights were off, and no interior illumination showed through the tinted glass windows.

Just as if the limo weren't there, I pulled Steve's van into the driveway, flipped on the inside lights, and examined Sammy and his crate for signs that he'd swallowed any sort of foreign object. Loose in the debris-packed Suburban, he might have eaten almost anything. Little

Sammy shared none of my anxiety. He wiggled in my arms, licked my face, tugged at my shoelaces, stuck his nose in his father's crate, and got a soft rumble in reply. The puppy crate was clean; Sammy had brought nothing up.

Still kneeling by the crate, I noticed the treasure that Sammy had carried in his mouth from the Suburban and dropped on the floor of the van. Now that the interior lights were on, I could see that the papers I'd glimpsed in the dark consisted of a glossy brochure and a letter printed on expensive business stationery. After a glance at the brochure, I knew exactly what it was and what it said, but I took a moment to read the letter in its entirety. The night was mild, the van was warm, and I was still wearing the denim jacket. Even so, a chill ran through me, not down my spine, either, but right down my throat to the pit of my stomach. The cause of the sensation was neither the contents of the letter nor the presence of Guarini's limo. Rather, it was what I tried to convince myself was the meaningless coincidence of the two: Guarini's car was *not* here because of the letter I'd just read. Yes, Enzio Guarini had the power to tap sources of information, but he was *not* clairvoyant. Until a few seconds ago, no one but little Sammy had known what he'd puppy-snatched from the Suburban, and he certainly didn't understand its significance. I did. I knew who'd killed Joey Cortiniglia. And I knew why.

When I unlocked and opened my back door, I found Enzio Guarini seated at my kitchen table. By now, it probably goes without saying that his bodyguards were

there, too. His trademark hat and walking stick lay on
the table. Rowdy and Kimi were still in the van. Sammy
was in my arms. I lowered him to the floor and watched
him run to Guarini, who bent to give the puppy a gentle
rubbing and then welcomed me home as graciously as if
the house were his and I were an eagerly awaited guest.

"Miss Winter," Guarini said, "it is always a pleasure."
His eyes crackled with life.

"Mr. Guarini. Good evening. Could I ask a favor?"

"I can hardly refuse. I'm here to ask one myself."

"Could you hang on to Sammy for a minute? I need
to get Rowdy and Kimi, and I don't want Sammy shoving
himself in Rowdy's face."

The presence of Guarini's limo felt like protection
against Deitz's threat against Rowdy and Kimi, but when
it comes to dogs, I hate to take chances. In that regard,
it's interesting to note that I had no hesitation about
entrusting Sammy to Guarini. At the same time, it never
occurred to me to report Zap's theft of Sammy to his boss.
Neither in that way nor in any other did I intend to enlist
Enzio Guarini as my hit man.

As I made the brief trip to the van and especially as I
passed through the kitchen with Rowdy and Kimi, I was
hideously aware of Sammy's paper treasure, which was
still in my pocket and, indeed, seemed to burn a hole
there, as money is said to do. When I reached my bedroom, where I intended to leave Rowdy and Kimi, I
stowed the Smith & Wesson on a high shelf in the closet,
but I left the papers in my pocket and kept the jacket
on.

I returned to the kitchen to find Sammy on the floor at Guarini's feet, where he was entertaining himself and the Dogfather by pulling at Guarini's shoelaces. The better to play with the puppy, Guarini had turned his chair away from the table. His bodyguards had turned with him. The foursome could have been posing for a surrealist photograph: Guarini, flanked by the frozen-faced men, with Sammy the puppy in weird contrast as he played riotous tug-of-war with the Mob boss's footwear.

"Could I offer you something?" I did not, of course, refer to a discourse about the allegory of Life and Death I was watching. "Wine? Coffee?"

After politely declining, Guarini said, "I've been giving a lot of thought to something you told me. About Frey. About dogs. It's something you been telling me all along about places."

"Places," I repeated.

"Dogs got close ties to places. Closer than us. If I learn a dance step"—he picked up the cane and twirled it—"once I got it, I can do it anywhere. But a dog, he's different. He learns heel here and now. Then he's in a different place, he's got to learn it all over again."

"Yes. Up to a point."

Guarini had let himself into my locked house to discuss canine generalization?

"So you got to wonder," he went on, "if the tricks, the dance steps, the behaviors, like you always say, are the part of it we notice because they're the things that interest us. Sit, stay, down, heel. But for a dog, maybe it's all like that, all wrapped up in places."

"You've lost me."

"Like memories."

"Probably. Yes, at a guess, a dog's whole consciousness, including memory, is fairly context specific, sort of glued to particular settings, objects, and so on."

"So like my favorite dog writer says, if you want to have a good shot at eliciting a behavior, go to the place the dog's used to showing it."

I smiled. "Both of my dogs are Obedience Trial Champions in our own backyard."

"Supposing you want to tap a dog's memory."

"Of a behavior?"

"Of something that happened. With people."

Still lost, I said, "The way you'd know that you'd tapped a memory would still be behavior. In other words, you'd read your dog."

Picking up his hat and his walking stick, Guarini rose. "I'm going to try a little experiment. Down behind that fancy health food store." With a sly narrowing of his eyes, he added, "Like in the movies, you know? A reenactment. You. Your dogs." Looking left and right, he said, "My associates here. A few other people."

"I don't have the same car. I'm borrowing a friend's van."

He shrugged. "Like I said, it's just a little experiment."

From the moment Guarini proposed the reenactment, I found the idea ridiculous. It occurred to me that prison had not only gotten to him, but gotten to him via a particular route: It had given him the chance to watch too many bad movies. But I didn't argue with him.

Consequently, the passage of only fifteen minutes found Rowdy, Kimi, and me at the scene of Joey Cortiniglia's murder, the parking lot behind Loaves and Fishes. Steve's van stood in for my defunct Bronco, and even though Sammy hadn't arrived in Boston at the time of the killing, he was now crated in it. Also, Joey Cortiniglia, being dead, obviously wasn't there. Still, Guarini seemed satisfied, and as I've already demonstrated all too fully, keeping Guarini happy was my principal, if unprincipled, goal throughout this affair. Somewhat to my surprise, Zap drove up in the Suburban with Al Favuzza, vampirish as ever, in the passenger seat. Finally, Carla Cortiniglia swept in behind the wheel of a pink Cadillac convertible so new looking that you could practically see the ghosts of dealer plates. Yes, a pink Caddy convertible. You see? No sign of Mob consciousness. If you happen to know an out-of-work political organizer, I know of a group that could use some serious help. Anyway, to protect her hairdo or to prevent Anthony from leaping out, Carla had the top up, and only after she'd emerged did I see her passengers, the gargantuan twins, Timmy and Tommy Bellano, who climbed out of the backseat with all the animation you'd expect from crash-test dummies who'd survived one nonaccidental accident and were about to be belted into another car to repeat the experience.

Carla's hair was big, and she wore a spray-on pink V-neck over white spray-on pants. Her heels were high, and she wore hoop earrings, gold bracelets, and her favorite fashion accessory, Anthony, whom she clutched in both hands as if he were a purse someone was trying to snatch. In the parking-lot lights, she and Anthony practically glowed in the dark. "Hi, there!" she greeted all of us. "You like my new car? Hey, Holly, I got to tell you, Anthony's doing great. You hear him? No barking. Silent as the grave. Oh, Jesus, what did I say? I need a zipper for my fat mouth."

Guarini nodded at Carla and then set about organizing the evening's event by directing the placement of the cars. Obedience-minded as I am, I'd already parked the van exactly where my Bronco had been, so I simply waited as Guarini had Favuzza moved the Suburban to the spot it had occupied. Meanwhile Zap drove the limo eight or ten spaces away and, as directed, parked it facing the front of the lot. Guarini asked Carla to park her convertible next to it. "Carla," Guarini said, "I got to ask you to leave Anthony in your car for a couple of minutes." As if he needed to soften or justify the request, he added, "I got Frey with me. He's going to stay in the car. Miss Winter, you're going to leave Sammy where he is, in your van, and you're going to act like he's not here."

Once Zap and Carla had carried out the instructions, I saw the point, which was to move both vehicles away from the area. Gesturing to Zap and Carla, Guarini gathered the whole group in a circle in the space between Steve's van and the Suburban. Although Joey Cortiniglia's bodily fluids and tissues were no longer visible on the blacktop, I could sense their traces underfoot and found myself shuffling and keeping the dogs on tight leads to shield my feet and their paws from contact with the dead. No one else showed a sign of sharing my superstition. Guarini and his guards stood where Joey's corpse had lain, and to their left, the Bellano twins leaned against the Suburban. Carla faced Guarini. She rested her weight on her right foot and, flexing her left ankle, tapped a slim heel in what struck me as a rhythm of courtship. To Carla's left was Zap, his arms folded across his scrawny chest. For once, his prematurely aged face bore an expression: He looked sullen. My dogs and I completed the circle, Rowdy on my left, Kimi on my right. Acknowledging Guarini as the alpha figure in the pack, the dogs watched his face in what I read as the vigilant expectation of a signal. We human beings silently waited for Guarini to speak. Remarkably, even Carla kept quiet.

It was typical of Guarini that he left unspoken what would have been a silly preamble about our wondering why he'd gathered us all together here. We knew why. Or everyone except Rowdy and Kimi did. Instead of wasting time voicing the obvious, that he wanted the name of Joey's killer, Guarini began by talking about dogs. Truly, the man was a mobster after my own heart. Pointing to Rowdy and Kimi, he said, "I got a lot of respect for malamutes. Smart. Strong. Natural. Beautiful. A lot like my elkhounds. But quieter."

Carla giggled. "Not like my Anthony!"

While Carla was still displaying the hysteria never observed in Alaskan malamutes or Norwegian elkhounds, Guarini turned to the bodyguard on his left. In expecting a signal, Rowdy and Kimi had been correct. As usual.

Anyway, the designated guard, who'd always seemed sur-
gically attached to Guarini, separated himself, stepped
forward, and, within seconds, was pressing an automatic
to Zap's chest. The guard's actions had been so smooth,
so professional, that I hadn't even seen him reach for the
weapon. Kimi, to my right, was next to Zap. She transferred her gaze from Guarini to me. Rowdy began to
watch her. Zap's face turned from a yellowish sallow to a
waxy green.

Guarini was smiling. "Miss Winter, supposing this was
you."

"Would my dogs protect me?"

He nodded.

"They'd have blocked access to me. Rowdy would definitely have done that."

"And supposing it was Joey."

"No. They probably wouldn't have done anything.
They wouldn't have barked or growled." Following Guarini's lead, I didn't bother to say that we weren't speaking
hypothetically. When Joey had been shot, my dogs hadn't
done a thing to protect him.

"So," said Guarini, "supposing Joey's here, and he's got
your dogs on leash, and somebody walks up to him."

"You know this already," I said. "It isn't that malamutes are bad guard dogs. What they are is non-guard
dogs. They take care of themselves. Rowdy and Kimi will
protect each other because in some ways they see each
other as one and the same, and for the same reason, they'll
watch out for me. But they're malamutes. They're never
going to act like mastiffs or Dobermans or shepherds . . .

or even like Anthony. Almost all the time, they love everyone, and they don't pretend otherwise."

"So Joey's here with two big dogs. These dogs, they look tough. And they're acting nice to Joey. And you don't know them and maybe you don't know Joey. And you see Joey and the dogs. What're you going to think?"

Carla answered. "Jesus! That they're Joey's dogs."

"If you're a stranger," I said, "you assume they'd defend him. Dogs this big and this tough can take bullets and keep going. And there are *two* dogs."

"This name I been hunting for," Guarini said. "It's the name of someone who knows something about dogs."

"It'd've been just like Blackie Lanigan to throw the dogs a bone," Favuzza said.

"How would he have known they weren't Joey's? How would he have known about my dogs?" I asked. "My particular dogs. I know this breed pretty well. Not every malamute is like mine. But every malamute has powerful jaws. I wouldn't take a chance with a malamute I didn't know."

"What else?" Guarini asked.

"Food," I answered. "Beef bones would be worth a try with most dogs and most breeds, but with Rowdy and Kimi, the bones were a guarantee of quiet, happy dogs."

"This name I been looking for," Guarini said, "I put the word out that I wanted the name. What I wanted was, I wanted to be wrong. I didn't want it to be one of the family. I didn't want it to be the name of one of you."

CHAPTER 29

Never take the word of a Mob boss. What Guarini staged wasn't a reenactment of Joey Cortiniglia's murder but a lineup of suspects before the only eyewitnesses to the crime, namely, Rowdy and Kimi. As a dog professional, I must comment that Guarini did an admirable job of seeing the killing from the dogs' point of view. He ignored the shooting to focus exclusively on the delectable beef bones that had been presented to my ever-ravenous dogs.

"We're going to reenact a little something here," said Guarini, referring, as I've just explained, to the dog-memorable event of the night Joey was slain rather than to the shooting itself. "Miss Winter here and me and Frey are over in front of the mall, and Zap, you, you're driving around like I told you." Guarini stared at Zap. "Maybe

you are. We're going to find out." Pointing at Zap, Guarini said, "You knew what Joey was delivering to me. Did
you get greedy? And with Joey out of the way, there's
more room for you to move up in the business. So, you
see this van here? You're going to move ten feet in front
of it. Turn your back to it. And stay there."

Zap obeyed. "Move to the right," Guarini directed.

"That's your left, you moron," Favuzza said. "Anyways
it was Blackie Lanigan."

Ignoring him, Guarini turned to the monster twins,
Tommy and Timmy Bellano. "You two. Same applies to
you. Greed's an awful thing. And like Miss Winter just
said about her dogs, there are two of you. You're out
patrolling the perimeter." Guarini swung his walking
stick in an arc. "Maybe. Go stand next to Zap. Stand just
like him."

When the Bellanos had taken their places in line,
Guarini turned to Al Favuzza. "Joey, he loves you like a
brother, Al. He respects you. He knows he's not as smart
as you. For you, it's easy. Joey trusts you. He does anything you tell him to do. I don't know what could've
made you betray Joey. But you're walking around keeping
an eye out. You're right nearby." Guarini pointed to Zap
and the twins. "Get in line, Al." And Al did.

Guarini's manner changed when he addressed Carla.
With a courtly tip of his hat, he said, "Carla, my dear."

"Me?" Carla said. "Me?" In my ears, but probably not
in Guarini's, she sounded startlingly like Miss Piggy:
Moi?

"You got a taste for the finer things," Guarini said.

From the lineup, his back still turned, Favuzza butted in. "Yeah, Carla, you're doing okay for yourself. Better than you'd ever would've done with Joey."

"Shut up, you goddamned vampire!" she shrieked. "I didn't know these dogs."

"You sure as shit knew they weren't Joey's, you cock-sucking little bitch," Al replied.

Guarini listened to the exchange with an air that I recognized from the canine world. It was the air of a dog with an agenda that eluded me, a dog who intended to steal a steak accidentally left on the counter, perhaps, but who was apparently paying attention to something else. Studying Guarini, I was hit by the sense that in staging this mini reenactment, this lineup, he had a purpose beyond the identification of Joey's killer. Worse, I had a tip-of-the-brain experience of almost being able to remember something crucial, something I knew and could all but retrieve, something amiss, although I had no idea of what, where, or when.

As Carla reluctantly took her place next to Al Favuzza, I wondered whether Guarini and his inseparable body-guards would join her—or maybe should join her. How long had I been in Loaves and Fishes on the night of Joey's killing? Kevin had pressed me for an answer. It seemed to me that I'd been inside long enough for Guarini or one of his escorts to have shot Joey and returned to the front of the store. But why would Guarini have surreptitiously killed one his own men and stolen his own money? I could think of a single reason: to lend credibility to his paranoia about Blackie Lanigan. If that were the case, though, why was he putting on tonight's performance?

Guarini did not take a place in the lineup. Instead, he told me to hitch my dogs to the front of the van exactly as they'd been hitched to my Bronco. I'd never before leashed a dog to an undercarriage, but I had no difficulty in getting Rowdy and Kimi to cooperate. In less than a minute, the dogs were just as I'd found them, with Kimi attached to the right front, Rowdy to the left. Without beef bones to occupy them, the dogs were now on their feet in front of the van, not lying on the blacktop as they'd been when Joey's body had lain only a few feet away.

Guarini nodded approval. "Just watch them. Move so you're not that close to them. And then, like you always say, read them."

Guarini's somewhat cryptic style of communication didn't bother me; I was used to creatures who didn't spell things out. His meaning was clear: Having positioned Rowdy and Kimi where they'd been when someone had given them beef bones, I was supposed to watch them for what might be subtle signs of expecting a repetition of that memorable act. Specifically, I was to look for any hint that my dogs' expectations centered on one of the five people in the lineup: Zap, Tommy, Timmy, Favuzza, and Carla. All five still faced away from the van, hence away from Rowdy and Kimi.

Guarini addressed his suspects: "What you're going to do in a minute, when I tell you, is you're going to turn around, and then you're going to take one step toward the dogs. And you're going to reach in your pockets, or make like you're reaching in your pockets, and you're going to bend a little and hold your hands out. And you're going to walk toward the dogs."

This rear parking lot was unpopular and almost deserted. A few people passed by and glanced at the odd scene, the row of people and the two beautiful dogs. No one approached. Oddity is so typical of Cambridge that it's practically the norm. The strangers probably thought that we were rehearsing an avant-garde play. I stopped looking around to concentrate on Rowdy and Kimi. Both dogs looked optimistic; they almost always did. As was usually the case, their ears were up, their eyes sparkled, their tails waved plumelike over their backs. The dogs' minds were easy to read. In their malamute lexicon, *optimism* didn't denote a globally sunny outlook; it meant the specific conviction that all human beings were here-and-now possessed of tremendous quantities of high-protein, high-fat delicacies destined for immediate delivery to the closest Alaskan malamutes. How do you read the happy expectation of food in dogs who perpetually expect it?

Guarini gave the order. "Turn around and move. Pretend like you got—"

Before he'd finished, Rowdy and Kimi hit the ends of their leads so hard that I was afraid they'd set the van in motion. Overjoyed, they hurled themselves toward Al Favuzza, who didn't bother to pretend that they'd picked out someone else.

"Who you going to believe?" Favuzza protested.

"They're just dogs, for Christ's sake. Who you going to believe? Me or some goddamned dogs?"

World's stupidest question. Guarini answered by pointing his walking stick at Tommy and Timmy Bellano, who understood the unspoken command and moved in on either side of Favuzza.

Never a man to disappoint a dog, Guarini said, "Miss Winter, you got liver on you? Give 'em some."

I complied. Then I unhitched the dogs one by one and crated them in Steve's van.

"Get him in my car," Guarini told the twins. To me, he said flatly, almost pleasantly, "Like you're always writing, if loyalty's what you want, get a dog."

Reaching into my pocket, I removed the puppy-chewed treasure that Sammy had found in the Suburban. I handed it to Enzio Guarini. "What started it," I said, "was my article. That's what gave him the idea. He read it, but I wrote it, so in a way, it's my fault."

Sammy's treasure: a glossy brochure from the mummification company I'd written about together with a letter to Alphonse Favuzza confirming the arrangements for his mummification. Al Favuzza's visit to the Museum of Fine Arts? The Boston MFA has room after room of outstanding exhibits from ancient Egypt. Favuzza's reaction when Joey's coffin was lowered into the earth? Favuzza wasn't grieved; he was sickened at the thought of bodily decay. He'd killed Joey and stolen Guarini's money to make sure that decomposition never happened to him.

CHAPTER 30

I'd seen enough Mafia movies to know what to expect next: Enzio Guarini and his associates would take Al Favuzza for a ride that would end when the concrete-shod Count took a plunge into Boston Harbor. As to me, the Dogfather would repeat what he'd said on the night Favuzza had killed Joey: He'd inform me that nothing had happened, and he'd tell me take my dogs and go home. I intended to take my dogs and leave, but my destination this time was going to be Cambridge Police Headquarters.

Anticipating Guarini's orders, I started to open the van door, but Guarini stopped me. "Stick around," he said. "I'll be right back. Carla, you get over here with Miss Winter, and you stay here. No matter what, you hear? *No matter what.*" Dog person that he was, he smiled at

me and said, "Yeah. Stand. Stay." Then, accompanied by
Zap and his bodyguards, he walked the short distance to
the limo. Zap held the door for him, and he vanished
behind the tinted windows. Zap got into the driver's seat
and closed the door. The headlights came on. The beams
shone across the asphalt toward the cars parked near the
front of the mall. If the engine started, I didn't hear it,
and the limo didn't pull forward toward the front of
Loaves and Fishes and the road beyond.

"Enzio's up to something," Carla said. "You can always
tell. He gets that funny smile. He's cute, huh? Old. But
cute. Don't you think he's kind of cute?"

Abandoning my dog-person abhorrence of cattiness, I
said, "Generous, too."

"Generous to a fault," Carla agreed. "Enzio's had a hard
life, you know. His wife passed away, and then his daughter, breast cancer, and—Oh, Jesus! Holy Jesus, look at
that!"

From Enzio Guarini's distinctive limousine emerged a
man wearing Guarini's trademark hat and carrying Guarini's trademark walking stick.

Carla repeated herself. "Jesus!"

"I doubt it," I said. Anyone less Christlike than Al
Favuzza was hard to imagine, and it had been Favuzza's
face I'd seen when the limo door had opened.

"What's he doing? Look what Al's doing! That's Al,
you know. That's not Enzio. He's walking in the headlights. Where's he going? Why's he doing it? Enzio
must've—"

"We're staying right here," I said. "Remember? No matter what. This is the *what*."

With Guarini's hat on his head and Guarini's stick in his hand, Favuzza moved in the beams of the headlights across the wide, empty stretch of asphalt at the side of the mall toward the cars parked in the front lot. Just as he was about to pass beyond the range of the headlights, he broke into a gawky sprint. Simultaneously, I not only heard but counted six gunshots that came not from Guarini's limo but from the opposite direction. In making a desperate, awkward attempt to run from death, Al Favuzza seemed to hurl himself head-on into the barrage of bullets, as if he were eagerly committing a grotesque form of suicide. His body spun, and before it had even hit the blacktop, I spotted a figure just beyond the distant row of parked cars, a familiar figure and, here in Cambridge, an ordinary one: a woman on a bicycle. Earlier this same evening when Guarini and I had sat in my kitchen discussing dogs and memory, I'd made the arrogant claim that we human beings enjoyed, or perhaps suffered from, a mental liberation from the constraints of space and time. Had I been right? If so, the sight of that very Cantabrigian woman here in the Loaves and Fishes parking lot proved that I was, indeed, half canine. The memory that had lingered on the tip of my brain was the memory of the woman who owned Kimi's dust mop with teeth. Like so many other residents of my neighborhood, the woman rode her bicycle, quoted Robert Frost and e. e. cummings, shopped at Loaves and Fishes, and otherwise blended so unobtrusively into Cambridge that she might as well not have been here at all.

Once a word moves from the tip of the tongue to the lips, it spits itself out in no time. That's how long it took Enzio Guarini's hidden army to emerge from fifteen or twenty apparently empty cars parked near the woman on the bicycle. Like wasps descending on a picnic, the men flew at the woman and swarmed over her. At a guess, twenty seconds had elapsed since the first gunshot. Carla was shrieking for Enzio, who now stepped out of his limo. To my surprise, he had Frey with him, and to my astonishment, he was not flanked by his bodyguards. Following Favuzza's route, Guarini moved quickly to the scene of the dust mop woman's capture. Carla started after him. So did I. If Guarini felt safe without the bodyguards, why should I hang back?

By the time I reached Guarini, the wasplike swarm of men had disappeared back into the cars and driven away. The woman lay on her stomach at Guarini's feet. Her ankles were bound with what I had no trouble in identifying as a leather dog leash. Behind her back, her arms were bound with a thin leather belt.

"Carla, my dear, be a nice girl and go get Anthony," Guarini said. When she'd tottered off on her high heels, he gave me one of those charming smiles of his. "Sit," he told Frey. The pup obeyed. "Good boy," Guarini told him. The praise was warm and genuine. Without a word to me, Guarini bent down, grabbed the prone, bound woman's head, and with a swift upward movement, removed her short, straight, ever-so-Cantabrigian gray hair.

The now-hairless woman twisted and squirmed. Holding Frey's leash in one hand and the wig in the other, Guarini just stood there smiling at me.

I started to say that I didn't understand. But all of a sudden, I did understand. The small flashlight I'd taken with me when I'd set out to rescue Sammy was still in my pocket. By its light, I saw the face of Guarini's captive. Everyone in Greater Boston knew that infamous face. Anyone else would've recognized it as easily as I did. We'd seen it in our newspapers and on our television screens. I'd seen it on the FBI website. I'd printed its image for Kevin Dennehy.

Enzio Guarini had captured Blackie Lanigan.

CHAPTER 31

When the police arrived, as they soon did, Enzio Guarini explained everything. The police had no choice about accepting his story. After all, he had proof. Blackie Lanigan was indubitably lying there in the parking lot with Guarini's belt around his wrists and Guarini's leather leash around his ankles. There was no question about whether Guarini and his girlfriend, Carla Cortiniglia, had, in fact, come to the area for an innocent session of dog training. He had the dogs and the dog trainer right there to support his statement. Carla bubbled about my success with Anthony. Guarini went so far as to demonstrate Frey's obedience for the cops, to whom he also offered a cogent explanation of clicker training. Frey behaved extremely well. I felt proud that he'd become the model puppy. With regard to Al Favuzza's body, now

minus the hat and walking stick, it was obvious that
Blackie Lanigan had made an attempt on Guarini's life
and shot the wrong man by mistake. "I'm lucky to be
alive," Guarini told the cops. He pointed to the weapon,
which was right there on the asphalt. It really was the
murder weapon, of course, and Blackie Lanigan really had
fired it.

It still infuriates me to realize that I'd seen that quintessentially Cantabrigian woman lots of times. Her dog
had attacked Kimi. I'd commented on her taste in novels.
In retrospect, I see the books as a give-away I missed.
The typical Cambridge type has already read Stephen
McCauley, Elinor Lipman, and Mameve Medwed. She
could've been rereading, of course, but if so, she should've
stopped to share her enthusiasm with me instead of pedaling off. In my obliviousness to her, I was like Mary
Wood with the heron that had killed her koi. Like the
heron, Blackie Lanigan had been there all along. Like
Mary, I just didn't know it.

Three days after Blackie Lanigan killed Al Favuzza, I
was finally allowed to visit Kevin Dennehy. The bullets
removed from Kevin's chest matched a gun found in Favuzza's apartment. "I knew it was that goddamned vampire, pardon my French," Kevin croaked. "I told you I
was nosing around. The stink was coming from Favuzza's
direction. They just wouldn't take the tubes out of my
throat so's I could talk."

Kevin was out of Intensive Care, but IVs and monitors
were strung around him like weird bird feeders around a
pale, sickly nestling. On his bedside table was a framed

photo of Blackie Lanigan. It was early evening, and we were watching a local TV special called "Here's Blackie."

"In a way," I told Kevin during a commercial, "Blackie succeeded in doing what Deitz tried and failed to do. Deitz's mistake was that he tried to enlist me as an informant. Also, he threatened my dogs. Blackie was smarter than that. He knew all about Guarini and dogs, he knew about Frey, and he kept an eye on Guarini. Once I was in the picture, Blackie planted himself in my vicinity. Kevin, you really have to admit that he picked the perfect disguise. And Guarini, for his part, set the whole thing up. He knew Blackie was out to get him. That wasn't just media hype. Guarini knew that Blackie was around somewhere, somewhere right nearby. He planted that whole army of his men in those parked cars. If my dogs had picked out Zap, or Timmy or Tommy Bellano, Guarini would've sent one of them across that parking lot instead. Guarini used Blackie to kill Joey's killer, and at the same time, he set things up so that when Blackie killed Joey's killer, Guarini would get Blackie."

"And Blackie fell for it."

"He'd been waiting for an opportunity. Guarini gave it to him. Guarini counted on Blackie to seize it. Blackie did."

The show resumed with footage of Enzio Guarini, who said that his true satisfaction came from bringing a notorious criminal to justice. The interviewer asked Guarini how he planned to spend the FBI's million-dollar reward for the capture of Blackie Lanigan. Guarini said that he was going to buy a second Norwegian elkhound. He also announced, right there on television, his engagement to Carla Cortiniglia. I didn't hear any more because Kevin's monitors went berserk, and a nurse rushed in and made me leave. Kevin's heart rate and blood pressure had abruptly risen. They dropped as soon as the nurse took my parting advice and turned off the television. I should never have let Kevin watch that special about Blackie in the first place. His body was still too weak to manage the stress.

Less than a week after my first hospital visit to Kevin, Steve returned from his mother's funeral. I explained why I'd thrown out the flowers. Then I went on to tell him everything.

"And this guy Favuzza's really gotten himself turned into a mummy?" Steve asked.

"He won't be a completed mummy for a while yet," I said. "It's long, complicated process. But yes. He paid to be mummified, so mummified he'll be. The mummification company must be delighted. They've done dogs and cats before, but Favuzza is their first human being. It's fitting, really, that he's the first. He honestly did have a horror of decomposition. Kevin told me that Favuzza's specialty was dirty work, but he didn't say exactly what kind. It turns out that it was moving buried bodies."

A few last things.

Guarini and I have never discussed Sammy's kidnapping, but I am sure that the boss found out about it because Rowdy got his chewman back, and it was returned not by Zap, but by Guarini himself.

I thought I'd never find out who blew up my car, and

it's true that I'll never be absolutely certain, but a short segment on the local evening news told me all I needed to know. It showed a pretty white colonial house in the suburb of Lexington. In the driveway sat the wreckage of a Ford station wagon that had been blown up. It belonged to a woman named Ellen Deitz. Her husband, Victor, worked for the FBI. It was a good bet that Deitz hadn't destroyed his wife's car. The television announcer suggested that the explosion might have been an act of revenge perpetrated by someone with a grudge against Victor Deitz in his capacity as an FBI agent. I agreed.

Speaking of cars, I still haven't replaced my Bronco, but I have a lead on a new car. A puppy-training client of mine says he can get me a great deal. Indeed, in the spirit of full openness about my association with the Mob, I have to confess that I have not yet entirely freed myself from Enzio Guarini. In fact, he called me only a few days ago. He remains grateful to me for everything. "I owe you one," said the Dogfather. "I owe you a big favor."